THE NEW
PURITANISM

THE NEW PURITANISM

PAPERS BY

LYMAN ABBOTT, AMORY H. BRADFORD
CHARLES A. BERRY, GEORGE A. GORDON
WASHINGTON GLADDEN, WM. J. TUCKER

DURING THE SEMI-CENTENNIAL CELEBRATION
OF PLYMOUTH CHURCH, BROOKLYN, N. Y.
1847–1897

WITH INTRODUCTION BY

ROSSITER W. RAYMOND

Essay Index Reprint Series

BOOKS FOR LIBRARIES PRESS
FREEPORT, NEW YORK

First Published 1897
Reprinted 1972

Library of Congress Cataloging in Publication Data
Main entry under title:

The New Puritanism.

   (Essay index reprint series)
   "First published in 1897."
   1. Puritans--Addresses, essays, lectures.
2. Theology--Addresses, essays, lectures.
I. Abbott, Lyman, 1835-1922. II. Brooklyn.
Plymouth Church.
BX9327.N46 1972   285'.9   70-39672
ISBN 0-8369-2732-X

PRINTED IN THE UNITED STATES OF AMERICA
BY
NEW WORLD BOOK MANUFACTURING CO., INC.
HALLANDALE, FLORIDA 33009

PUBLISHERS' PREFACE.

THE expansion both of knowledge and of wisdom in all departments of life during the Nineteenth Century has nowhere been more manifest than in religious matters. The general mental attitude in nearly all communions has changed, towards God and towards man. The result is an immense increase of vital interest, with a corresponding decline in mere formalism.

This is particularly noticeable in two directions. One is that, where formerly the more conscientious professing Christians would "read a chapter" in the Bible with a comfortable sense of duty done, now thousands, Christians and others, are studying those ancient scriptures with discrimination, yet with genuine delight in their treasures —of allegory, of biography, of history, of literature, of spiritual instruction and inspiration. Whether as cause or as consequence, is the other: that the pregnant practical teachings of the Master himself are looked to for "standards" of faith and doctrine, rather than the ingenious speculations of his followers, however saintly or learned.

Jesus had no time for rhetoric. His brief sayings are compact of germinant life. One of them—perhaps as characteristic of his whole career as any—is that "The Sabbath was made for man, not man for the Sabbath." The principle involved in this maxim is that which has developed into the splendid humanitarianism of Christian life and work to-day: although its full meaning is yet to appear.

Like all the enlargement of the physical and psychical sciences during the past century, the religious growth has been greatest —or by reason of multiplied ramifications most discernible—within the latter half of that period. It was natural, then, that the fiftieth anniversary of the inauguration of so

potent an influence as Plymouth Church and
the coming of its first pastor should offer
an occasion for reviewing at large the vast
spiritual migration of multitudes of Christian pilgrims to "fresh fields and pastures
new." And the occasion would lack its
best worth if this did not include a look
forward to coming duties and privileges.
During that celebration, therefore, both
retrospect and prospect—the past century
and the coming one—were set forth by
men of acknowledged eminence, whose
broad views will attract and interest thinking people. It was inevitable that the
speakers should find special concern with
Henry Ward Beecher and Plymouth Church;
not, however, merely because these were at
the focal point of the occasion, but because
in any consideration of morals and religion
in America during the past half-century " he
reckons ill who leaves [them] out."

The Addresses pertaining to the celebration have been gathered into this volume.
Concerning the particular relations of the

speakers to that church and its first pastor, as well as to the themes assigned them, the publishers are glad to present an introductory paper from Dr. R. W. Raymond,—for forty-two years a member of the church, an intimate friend of both the first and the present pastor, and a recognized leader in the brotherhood, not only intellectually and spiritually, but in the practical organization and administration of the work of the church.

The larger bearings of these Addresses— those indeed for which they were mainly planned and of which they chiefly and ably treat—will be evident from their titles, and still more from their admirable contents.

TABLE OF CONTENTS.

Introductory.

ROSSITER W. RAYMOND.

INTRODUCTORY.

THE occasion, though not directly the topic, of the addresses contained in this volume was the semi-centennial jubilee of Plymouth Church. The story of the origin of the church, as briefly outlined in the *Outlook* of Nov. 13, 1897, is as follows:

" A Brooklyn merchant had accidentally heard Henry Ward Beecher in Indianapolis, and the hearing had aroused his desire to bring the almost boyish preacher to New York. The unsuspecting candidate for the pulpit of a not yet existing church was invited to deliver an address before one of the missionary societies at the then famous May meetings. He came east for this purpose. Meanwhile, a few gentlemen interested in this Christian conspiracy met at a private house on the 8th of May, 1847, and decided then and there to purchase a church building on Cranberry Street, which the First Presbyterian Church had just vacated, in order to follow the population to a more favorable location upon the Heights. A week later (May 16, 1847) Henry Ward Beecher preached in this church building his first sermon in Brooklyn. Plymouth Church, however, was not organized until nearly a month later (June 13) ; the following day, Mr. Beecher was called to its pastorate, but did not accept the call until August; he began his labors on October 10, and was installed by Council Nov. 11.''

This series of events was followed approximately in the recent celebration, which comprised :

1. A memorial prayer-meeting of the church, held Friday evening, May 7, in commemoration of the original conference of May 8, 1847.

2. Services on Sunday, May 16, the fiftieth anniversary of Mr. Beecher's first sermon in Brooklyn. In the morning, Rev. Lyman Abbott, D.D., pastor of Plymouth Church, preached on '' The New Puritanism''; in the evening, Rev. Amory H. Bradford, of Montclair, N. J., preached on '' Puritan Principles and the Modern World.''

3. Services on Sunday, November 7, at which Rev. Charles A. Berry, D.D., of

Wolverhampton, England, preached morning and evening, his theme in the morning being "The Influence of Henry Ward Beecher's Teaching on Religious Life and Thought in England," and in the evening "The Secret of the Power of the Christian Church." The morning service was followed by the administration of the Lord's Supper.

4. On Thursday evening, November 11, the fiftieth anniversary of the installation of Henry Ward Beecher, a service at which addresses were made by Rev. George A. Gordon, D.D., of Boston, Mass., on "The Theology for To-day"; by Rev. Washington Gladden, D.D., on "The Social Problems of the Future"; and by Rev. William J. Tucker, D.D., President of Dartmouth College, on "The Church of the Future."

5. On Friday evening, November 12, a prayer-meeting of the church, to express gratitude for the past and renewed consecration for the future.

Concerning the distinguished speakers

named above, little need be said to explain the invitation extended to them by Plymouth Church. The wisdom of that invitation is vindicated by the results here gathered for publication.

Dr. Bradford is a friend of many years, to Plymouth Church, to Mr. Beecher, and to Mr. Beecher's successor, and his splendidly earnest and active church in Montclair contains many emigrants from Plymouth, who have found themselves in no strange atmosphere by reason of their change of residence. His work and his books have caused him to be recognized as a representative Christian pastor, as well as teacher.

Dr. Berry, by virtue of official position as well as of acknowledged eminence, may claim to speak for the Congregational churches of the country where Congregationalism originated, and therefore to measure truly and report fairly the progress and tendency of those bodies. But he is dear to Plymouth for other reasons. He was not yet thirty-five years of age when Henry

Ward Beecher, deeply impressed with his eloquence, invited him to visit America, and preach in Plymouth Church. The invitation was accepted; but Mr. Beecher's death intervened before the promise given could be fulfilled. When, after several months, the young minister came, his personal magnetism and apostolic fervor found instant recognition, and he received an enthusiastic call to the Plymouth pulpit. This call, which, after due consideration, he declined, was followed by a widened sphere of activity and fame in his own country: and after the lapse of a decade, Plymouth Church was glad to welcome again, in the vigor of his prime, him whom it had loved in his ardent youth. The urgent requests pressed upon him from every quarter, during his six weeks' stay in this country, and the interest excited by his numerous public addresses during that period, in New York, Montclair, New Haven, Boston, Chicago, Washington, etc., have confirmed the reputation he had already gained among American Christians.

Dr. Gordon, whose ministrations in the historic Old South Church of Boston, not less than his published lectures and essays, have put him in the forefront among modern theological thinkers, was preëminently qualified to clothe the old faith in the terms of the new philosophy.

Dr. Gladden, identified not only with liberal conceptions of Christian truth, but yet more with liberal applications of it to modern social needs, was the fit mouthpiece for the Divine message, calling the church of Christ to wider fields and fresh endeavors.

President Tucker was the author of a notable address delivered some years ago before the Phi Beta Kappa Association of Harvard University, and one of the inspirers and founders of that " Andover House " which is to-day, under a different name, doing in the city of Boston a practical work for Christ, and has set the example for the similar work carried on by Union

Theological Seminary in the city of New York. These and other services marked him as a prophet, bearing a word of the Lord concerning the church of the future.

A simple inspection of this list of orators and topics will show that the semi-centennial jubilee of Plymouth Church was not planned to be a glorification of its history, or of its beloved first pastor, or of his successor. Indeed, these causes for pride and gratitude are so vividly and perpetually present in the consciousness of its members, that they do not need to be recalled by formal celebration. It was deemed a worthier use of the occasion to devote it largely to the recognition and declaration of the ideals toward which the church is striving in its inner life and outward activities, to the demonstration of its agreement in this faith and practice with the working churches of two continents, to the contemplation of its own duties, present and future, and to a solemn self-consecration for yet higher and more fruitful service.

That this was the fittest commemoration of Henry Ward Beecher's life and work, no one familiar with the history of Plymouth Church for the past ten years can doubt. It is well known that, at the time of Mr. Beecher's death, few persons outside of the church believed that it could continue to be what, under the inspiration of his leadership, it had been. Besides those less friendly observers, who, deeming it but a heterogeneous assemblage, held together by the magnetism of one man, prophesied that it would fall to pieces when his presence was withdrawn, there were among its sympathizing friends few, if any, who did not sorrowfully anticipate at least some measure of retreat, some diminution of activity, some loss of power, some partial surrender of the field of work, perhaps a necessary change of locality, involving almost a practical sacrifice of the continuity and identity of the life of the church. Such apprehensions were natural enough to those who did not understand what had been the real result of Henry Ward Beecher's pastoral work of forty years. He had recruited and organized, trained and disciplined and led an army of Christian soldiers, which did not dream of retreating or surrendering or disbanding because its captain had fallen on the field. The church was neither a crowd, fascinated by oratory, nor a throng of friends, held by loving admiration of their friend, nor a philanthropic society, trying a benevolent experiment, and dependent upon advertising and popular support. It was an organized body of working Christians— "heterogeneous" indeed, as a church ought to be, and held together by loyalty to one person; but that person was the living, present Lord Jesus Christ. A striking and conclusive proof of the truth of this proposition is the fact that although, ten years ago, the surrounding air was laden with predictions and suggestions of retreat, no word of that kind was heard from within the church. In its crowded meetings, no voice intimated fear of failure. Its animated discussions all terminated in practically unanimous decisions. The writer, as chairman of the Advisory Committee of the church during this period of its fancied peril, had ample opportunity to know the temper of his brethren, and bears joyful testimony to their unswerving, undaunted, and undivided enthusiasm of service.

Ten years have proved that this enthusiasm was not a flash, but a glow. Plymouth Church, originally established in a locality abandoned as unfavorable to such an enterprise, still holds its post, finding its warrant in the work which lies about its doors. Some of its members come many miles to their worship and labors—the average distance considerably exceeds a mile. Yet not one of the branches of church-work established by Mr. Beecher has been discontinued; and new ones have been added to the list. The social and the spiritual life of the church are undiminished in vigor; and it still enjoys abundant comment and advice from the newspapers, which may be taken as evidence that it still exerts an influence upon the community.

Certainly this survival of a church supposed to be doomed to decline or decay is a phenomenon worth noting; and it is fair to presume that the Divine blessing, to which, above all, success has been due, has been bestowed upon the continued preaching of what Dr. Berry calls " the credible and beautiful gospel " of which Mr. Beecher was an apostle, upon Christian lives inspired by that teaching, and upon conceptions and methods of church-work suited to the conditions and demands of our time.

The services connected with the late semi-centennial jubilee, taken together, presented a comprehensive picture of such a church as Plymouth has been or aims to become. Perhaps the most characteristic features of this picture were those which are not included in the present volume—the testimony, the aspiration, the brotherly love, expressed in the prayer-meetings of the church itself. Nor should it be inferred that the addresses here given constitute a formal and official programme of this church. Nevertheless, they do express, with individual variety and freedom, the general standpoint and attitude of Plymouth Church, present, past, and future. It has stood for liberty and progress in theological thought; for the application of the principles and precepts of Jesus Christ to social questions as well as to single lives; and for the right and duty of the church to employ all measures and all instruments which can be consecrated to the service of God and of humanity. It has welcomed the light, and followed its kindly leading. It has tried to do Christ's work, in Christ's way, in his name, and with his help. And to this high calling it now gratefully girds itself anew.

R. W. RAYMOND.

BROOKLYN, November 27, 1897.

The New Puritanism.

LYMAN ABBOTT.

I.

The New Puritanism.[1]

By LYMAN ABBOTT, D.D.,
Of Plymouth Church, Brooklyn, N. Y.

And he gave some, apostles; and some,
prophets; and some, evangelists; and some, pas-
tors and teachers; for the perfecting of the
saints, for the work of the ministry, for the
edifying of the body of Christ: till we all come
in the unity of the faith, and of the knowledge
of the Son of God, unto a perfect man, unto the
measure of the stature of the fulness of Christ.
—*Ephesians*, iv : 11, 12, 13.

FIFTY years ago to-day, in this very
place, though not in this building, Henry
Ward Beecher preached his first sermon in
Brooklyn. That fact suggests the text and

---

[1] Plymouth Church, Sunday morning, May 16, 1897.
Reported by Henry Winans; revised by the author.

the theme for this occasion. I am not going, however, to preach a sermon of reminiscences, nor to speak to-day to the older members of Plymouth Church. I am somewhat doubtful about the value of such reminiscences, somewhat doubtful about the value of endeavoring to live over the past. A generation has grown up who do not know that past, who do not know out of what the Church of Christ has come into its present light and life and liberty, and who are not, therefore, able to discern the tendencies of to-day, because they do not understand the history of yesterday. It is to this generation I speak this morning, for the purpose of pointing out to them, as well as I can within the limits of a discourse not to be unduly prolonged, what has been that transition from the old Puritanism to the new Puritanism, in which, as I think, Mr. Beecher and Plymouth Church have taken no inconsiderable part.

John Calvin declared that man had lost his freedom in the Fall; he was no longer

a free moral agent.' Whatever else may
be said respecting Calvinism, it was at least
logical and self-consistent, and the doctrine
of John Calvin, incorporated in the Westminster Confession of Faith, remains there
to the present day. Jonathan Edwards in
the middle of the last century gave philo-
sophic exposition to the dogmatic declaration of Calvin.² He possessed what Calvin
lacked—a spiritual imagination. He was
philosopher rather than dogmatist. His
argument in his famous treatise on the
Freedom of the Will may be put very
tersely—at least for the purposes of this
morning: Every phenomenon has its cause;
therefore, said Edwards, every volition of
the will must have a cause. The man's
will is controlled, as everything else is con-

---

¹ " Man is not possessed of free will for good
works, unless he be assisted by grace, and that
special grace which is bestowed on the elect alone in
regeneration."—*Calvin's Institutes*, vol. II. p. 238.

² The reader who has not time to read Jonathan
Edwards' Works will find a full and sympathetic,
though critical, interpretation of them in **Dr. A. V. G,**
Allen's *Life of Jonathan Edwards.*

trolled. He must decide according to the strongest motive; because if he did not decide according to the strongest motive, then he would decide according to a motive weaker than the stronger, and that is a self-contradiction. Man therefore has no freedom of the will. Freedom—so Jonathan Edwards argued—consists in power to *do* what you will; it does not consist in power to *will* what you will do. The power which Chrysostom affirmed in the will, to choose between good and evil, Jonathan Edwards explicitly and in terms denied. This denial was the crucial point, the foundation-doctrine of the old Puritanism. Man had lost his freedom; he was no longer able to choose the right and eschew the wrong; he could not repent; he could not do virtuous deeds; he could not accept God's grace; he could do nothing. But God in his infinite mercy was pleased to rescue some men from this state of servitude. He was not pleased to rescue all; he was not under any obligation to rescue any. Man was culpable, although he could not choose. God was pleased by a miraculous act of grace to select some men and take them out of this bondage, this life of servitude, and put them into a new life. These men were the chosen; they were God's elect. The men whom God had not chosen thus to select and rescue by a miraculous act of grace were hopelessly and eternally lost. Man himself had no more power to repent and begin a new life than Lazarus had to come forth out of his tomb before Christ had said to him, Lazarus, arise! and no more power to stay unrepentant, when Christ had called him to repentance, than Lazarus would have had to remain in the sleep of death after Christ had said, Lazarus, come forth! The grace that summoned men was an irresistible grace. If summoned they could not help but come, and not one could come unless so summoned.

In the old Puritanism this was not an abstract doctrine, held only by metaphysicians and confined to scholastic discussion.

It was embodied in the practical ministry
of the churches in the earlier history of
New England. A simple extract from a
practical sermon by an eminent preacher of
New England of the seventeenth century,
the Rev. Thomas Shepherd, one of the
founders of Harvard College, will illustrate
this. Imagine it preached to-day in the
chapel of that university:

" Oh thou mayest wish and desire to come
out sometime, but canst not put strength to thy
desire, nor indure to doe it. Thou mayest hang
down thy head like a Bulrush for sin, but thou
canst not repent of sin; thou mayest presume,
but thou canst not beleeve; thou mayest come
half way, and forsake some sins, but not all
sins ; thou mayest come & knock at heaven
gate, as the *foolish virgins* did, but not enter in
and passe through the gate; thou mayest see
the land of *Canaan*, & take much pain to goe
into *Canaan*, and mayest tast of the bunches of
Grapes of that good land, but never enter into
Canaan, into Heaven, but thou liest bound hand
and foot in this woful estate, and here thou
must lie and rot like a dead carkasse in his
grave, untill the Lord come and rowle away the
stone, and bid thee come out and live." [1]

[1] Quoted in *Some Aspects of the Religious Life of
New England*, by George Leon Walker, D.D., p. 23.

This doctrine is no longer preached in our churches; but it is still preserved in some of our creeds. Its philosophy is embodied in that Westminster Confession of Faith, which we might all be glad to recognize as an honest and able attempt in the seventeenth century to systematize religious philosophy, but which we must declare to be heresy when men still demand adhesion to it as the best embodiment possible in our times, of the glorious Gospel of Jesus Christ. This is what the Westminster Confession of Faith declares on this subject,—that Confession of Faith which is accepted for substance of doctrine by a very considerable proportion of the religious teachers of this country, and is even exalted to be a standard of faith by some Congregational ministers:

"Works done by unregenerate men, although for the matter of them they may be things which God commands, and of good use both to themselves and others; yet because they proceed not from a heart purified by faith, nor are done in a right manner, according to the Word, nor to a

right end, the glory of God; they are therefore
sinful, and cannot please God, or make a man
meet to receive grace from God.   And yet their
neglect of them is more sinful and displeasing
unto God." [1]

The Psalmist had said, " He that hath
clean hands and a pure heart, who hath not
lifted up his soul unto vanity, nor sworn
deceitfully, he shall receive the blessing
from the Lord, and righteousness from the
God of his salvation.''   But the old Puritanism said No! Though he wash his hands,
though he cleanse his life, though he walk
according to his conscience, this is not
a ground on which he can receive grace
from God.   The prophet Isaiah had said:
" Let the wicked forsake his way, and the
unrighteous man his thoughts: and let him
return unto the Lord, and he will have
mercy upon him, and to our God, for he
will abundantly pardon.''   But the old
Puritanism declared that that was only said
in order to deepen the despair of men, for

---

[1] *West. Conf. of Faith*, ch. XVI, § vii.

no unrighteous man can forsake his evil way, and no wicked man can abandon his evil thoughts.

Thus a system of fatalism had grown up and been wrought out in the old Puritanism, as absolutely fatalistic as the modern Necessarianism. The old Puritanism said, as modern Necessarianism says, that man is the creature of his heredity and of his environment, but it added that they are both hopelessly bad. It declared that man is the son of a fallen race, and has inherited nothing but depravity from his parents; is a member of a fallen race, and is surrounded by nothing but depravity in the community. He is the creature of his heredity, and that is depraved; he is the creature of his environment, and that is depraved; there is no hope for him, unless by a miraculous act of supernatural power he is taken out of his heredity and out of his environment: and whether this miraculous grace will thus rescue any particular man or not, no man can tell. Nothing that he can do, nothing

that any one can do for him, will help or
hasten this miraculous process.

As to infants there was a hot debate,
which, so far as the Westminster Confession
of Faith was concerned, was settled by a
compromise—by the declaration that elect
infants dying in infancy are saved, leaving
those who thought there were no elect
infants to say they are not elect, and those
who thought that all infants are elect to say
they are all saved, and those who thought
that some are elect and some not, to say
that some are saved and some not. It was
one of the cases in which words were used
not in a double but in a triple sense, and
each man might take the meaning he pre-
ferred.

This old Puritanism, fatalistic in the very
essence of its philosophy, of course regarded
religion as something unnatural. It did
not belong to man's nature. It was something outside and beyond him. It was,
therefore, something outside and beyond
reason. As he could not arrive at righteous-

ness by any obedience to law, so he could not arrive at truth by any exercise of his reason. Religion was wholly supernatural, not to say contranatural, and depravity was wholly natural. Truth was wholly the result of a supernatural revelation, and no man could arrive at truth except it were supernaturally revealed to him, not only by the Bible, but by a supernatural grace accompanying the Bible. It was not enough that he had the Bible, and that he had preachers to interpret the Bible, and a natural inclination to accept the teachings of the Bible; he must have in addition miraculous light streaming down upon him from God on the pages of the Bible and into his heart and his understanding, or the truth and the desire to understand and receive and obey the truth were all of no avail, for he had not any capacity to perceive or understand or receive the truth except as it was supernaturally bestowed upon him in regeneration. The light of nature was not enough, nor the Bible enough, nor these two enough, even when aided by some "common operations of the Spirit." Upon this point the Westminster Confession of Faith is as explicit as upon the others. Indeed, the two are logically and necessarily connected:

"Others, not elected, although they may be called by the ministry of the Word, and may have some common operations of the Spirit, yet they never truly come unto Christ, and therefore cannot be saved; much less can men not professing the Christian religion be saved in any other way whatsoever, be they never so diligent to frame their lives according to the light of nature and the law of that religion they do profess; and to assert and maintain that they may is very pernicious and to be detested." [1]

This fatalistic religion did not accomplish that which has been claimed for the old Puritanism. In the beginning of the present century intemperance was common — far more common than to-day, not only outside the church, but inside the church; and, according to the testimony of Dr. Lyman Beecher, at ordination services the side-

---

[1] *West. Conf. of Faith,* ch. x, § iv.

board of the pastor looked and smelled like
the bar of a grog-shop; and he adds: " None
of the Consociation were drunk; but that
there was not, at times, a considerable
amount of exhilaration, I cannot affirm."[1]
Slavery was extending its black cloud over
one half the continent, and the Church, at
the beginning of the present century, was

---

[1] " At the ordination at Plymouth, the preparation
for our creature comforts, in the sitting-room of Mr.
Heart's house, besides food, was a broad sideboard
covered with decanters and bottles, and sugar, and
pitchers of water. There we found all the various
kinds of liquors then in vogue. The drinking was
apparently universal. This preparation was made by
the society as a matter of course. When the Consociation arrived, they always took something to
drink round; also before public services, and always
on their return. As they could not all drink at once,
they were obliged to stand and wait as people do
when they go to mill. There was a decanter of
spirits also on the dinner-table, to help digestion,
and gentlemen partook of it through the afternoon
and evening as they felt the need, some more and
some less; and the sideboard, with the spillings of
water, and sugar, and liquor, looked and smelled
like the bar of a very active grog-shop. None of the
Consociation were drunk; but that there was not, at
times, a considerable amount of exhilaration, I cannot affirm."—*Autobiography of Lyman Beecher*, vol. I.,
ch. xxxvii., p. 245.

generally silent. Dr. Hopkins of brave memory raised his voice against slavery: but then Dr. Hopkins was not orthodox— he was also at the same time writing two volumes entitled *The New Divinity.* The heresy and the moral reform were going along together. There were no missionary organizations, either home or foreign; and when first the attempt was made to organize a foreign missionary organization, the preachers of fatalism protested against it as an irreverent attempt to interfere with the decrees of Almighty God.

Of course this system was not without some compensating advantages. It did develop in men a profound sense, if a somewhat morbid sense, of their guilt and sinfulness; it did develop in men a very profound, if not altogether healthful, reverence for God. If reverence be compounded, as the philosophers tell us it is, partly of fear and partly of love, then we must say that the reverence of the old Puritanism was mostly fear and very little love. But still there was reverence, and by it the conscience was made strong, and when the conscience was brought to bear on human life it carried with it tremendous sanction. There were revivals of religion also; but the revivals of religion were generally emotional rather than ethical. They were transitions from a state of indifference, through a state of despair and a state of exhilaration, into a state of peace. Jonathan Edwards, in his book or essay on Revivals, gives five tests of a work of grace. They are these: first, increased esteem for Christ; second, diminution of worldliness—by which he means dancing, card-playing, and the like; third, respect for the Scriptures; fourth, reception of the truth—by which he means the New England system of theology; and fifth, love. If by " love " he had meant what in these later days we mean, we might have accepted it as an adequate interpretation of Christ's saying: " By their fruits ye shall know them." But he does not mean by " love " what we mean by " love "; he does not define it as Christ defines it in the parable of the Good Samaritan, and as Paul defines it in the thirteenth chapter of First Corinthians. Love, he says, is spurious unless it is " attended with a sense of our own unworthiness, as in ourselves the enemies and haters of God and Christ, and with a renunciation of all our excellency and righteousness." Any one who will compare the account of the revivals of religion under Jonathan Edwards, in 1740, and the revivals of religion under Dr. Finney, in the early part of this century, will see the radical ethical difference between the two. The system of theology which openly scorned what Dr. Lyman Beecher called the " natural virtues " was not adapted to do much toward eradicating " natural vices." After one of Dr. Finney's sermons in Oberlin, the people of the town were seen the next morning going about the village returning the books and saws and axes which they had borrowed. No such sign of revival was ever witnessed, I venture

to say, under the preaching of the old
Puritanism.

Already before the beginning of this century the old Puritanism had created a
reaction. We seem to swing, like a pendulum, back and forth, and never stay
stationary in the center. This reaction was
seen in several ways. First, in a blatant,
irreverent, blasphemous, and unintelligent
infidelity. Thomas Paine's *Age of Reason* was finally given to the public in the
year 1795. While, of course, some of its
statements are accepted to-day — for no
man, however great his genius, can write a
book of one hundred pages and not say
some true things—on the whole, Paine's
attitude of mind is repudiated by all un-
believers of the present time, unless possibly I except Robert Ingersoll. But when
it was published Paine's *Age of Reason* was,
perhaps, the most popular book of the time.
When President Dwight took the presi-
dency of Yale College, it is said that there
were only four professing Christians in the

whole College and two Thomas Paine societies; and so popular was French infidelity
that a number of leading members of the
senior class had dropped their own names
and taken as their own, those of leading
French infidels.[1]

The second reaction was the great Methodist movement. The Methodism which
was born in England in the middle of the
eighteenth century had spread to the United
States before its close. It denied emphati-
cally the fatalism of Calvin and Edwards
with the accompanying doctrine of particular election, and affirmed in the most vig-
orous manner the freedom of volition and
the universal provision of divine grace. It
transferred responsibility for the moral action of the individual from God to man,
and in this was its power; it passed by, if
it did not ignore, the sovereignty of law
and the Lawgiver over free moral agents,
and in that was its weakness.

---

[1] *Life of Timothy Dwight:* Introduction to *Dwight's
Theology*, p. 20.

This movement was followed by one more local in its character, the Unitarian revolt, in the beginning of the present century. It was confined to the Puritan churches and, in the main, to those of New England origin. Under the leadership of Channing it denied the Trinity, but not the divinity of Christ. Rather, it affirmed the inherent divinity of man. It did not stop with declaring that man preserved freedom of volition; it also declared the excellence of the "natural virtues" which Puritanism condemned, and affirmed the practical and ethical and natural character of religion. Says its great leader, Dr. Channing: "I conceive these to be the leading principles of modern divinity: practical righteousness is all in all, and every system which embraces motives enough to a good practice is sufficiently correct. *Love* is the fulfilling of the law and of the gospel. All truth is designed to excite this temper, and to form the habits which flow from it, and this is the only test which we fallible mortals can apply to doctrines.''

More important than either Methodism or Unitarianism, from the theological point of view, was that revival of philosophy which may be traced back to Samuel Taylor Coleridge (1816–1834), in the first quarter of the present century, though it includes among its apostles such men as Erskine of Scotland, Maurice and Stanley in England, Bushnell and Phillips Brooks in America. Coleridge parted from the old Puritanism in his fundamental conception of both man and religion: man possesses a free determining creative will, which is the secret of his spiritual, godlike nature. If he has not this he is a machine, not a man: neither amenable to moral law nor capable of moral virtue. Religion is the supreme life of this will, its highest development, and so man's highest education. Religion therefore rests, in the last analysis, not upon an authority without,— whether of church, creed, or Bible,—but upon the reason and conscience

of man, upon his own spiritual recognition
of and deference to divine law and divine
truth. If he has not a natural capacity to
perceive and receive the truth he has no
capacity for religion, and is a mere higher
animal, not a man.

Crossing the ocean and following the less
philosophical and more emotional protest of
Methodism and the less spiritual but more
purely ethical protest of Unitarianism, both
of which had prepared for its advent, this
rational and spiritual philosophy of life
mixed with and modified the Old Puritanism, making of it a New Puritanism. In
the transition from the Old to the New such
theological teachers as Edwards A. Park,
such revival preachers as Charles G. Finney,
such mediators between the rationalist and
the scholastic theologian as Dr. Lyman
Beecher and Albert Barnes and Horace Bushnell, were efficient and representative factors.
They differed widely in temperament, and
materially in philosophy; but they agreed
in insisting on man's free will, or his natural

ability to choose the right and eschew the
wrong; on man's personal responsibility for
his choice, as well as for his outward actions;
on the naturalness of religion and man's
native, inherent capacity for it; and on the
natural virtues as the sole satisfactory evidence of the possession of supernatural
grace. For this teaching, now so elemental
in Congregational theology, Drs. Park, and
Finney, and Kirk, and Lyman Beecher,
and Horace Bushnell, and Mr. Barnes were
all accused of heresy, and Dr. Lyman
Beecher and Mr. Barnes were put on trial
in the Presbyterian Church, with, as a
result, the division in 1838 of the great
Presbyterian Church into two churches,
each maintaining the same General Confession, but one interpreting it according to
the Old Puritanism, the other according to
the New. The first was historically accurate, but was unscriptural and unphilosoph-
ical; the second was scripturally and philo-
sophically accurate, but departed widely

from the traditional theology and historic standards of the Church.

The ethical reaction against the Old Puritanism was quite as marked as the theological reaction. The temperance movement, though by no means confined to the Puritan churches, received its impulse and its consecration therefrom. In fifteen years after Lyman Beecher preached his "six sermons against intemperance" the consumption of strong drink in New England had decreased more than one half *per capita*. In the Puritan churches, if we may include the Unitarian offshoots from Puritanism, and in the Friends' Meetings, the antislavery movement also received its chiefest religious impulse, and almost exclusively in the churches of the New Puritanism. The Old School Church was an apologist if not a defender of slavery. The Congregational churches which adhered to the Edwardsian theology were never found in the skirmish-line, and rarely in attacking column, of either the temperance or the antislavery forces, while

Lyman Beecher and Charles G. Finney, and
Edwards A. Park, and Horace Bushnell,
and Albert Barnes were all equally known
as reformers in the moral life and in theological philosophy.

This rapid historical survey seemed to be
necessary to make possible an intelligible
picture of the conditions of life and thought
in 1847, when Henry Ward Beecher, in the
thirty-fourth year of his age, preached his
first sermon in Brooklyn in the place,
though not in the church-building, where
we are now gathered.

The Old Puritanism was still dominant.
Whether we measure force by numbers,
wealth, or social eminence, we must accord
to the Old Puritanism the first place. Still,
Lyman Beecher, Dr. Finney, Dr. Bushnell, Mr. Barnes and Professor Park were
making the churches familiar with the then
new but now axiomatic doctrine that man
is free, that religion is natural to him, and
that all virtue is acceptable and all vice
blamable in regenerate and unregenerate

alike. The Mexican War was drawing to its close; the cannon thundering on Mexican plains was awaking the sluggish conscience of New England to a sense of its participation in and responsibility for slavery. Theodore Parker had just begun his campaign against it in Boston. Garrison was at once provoking by his unwisdom and overcoming by his courage the prejudices and the passions of conservative New England. John G. Whittier was writing now editorials, now poems, to awaken the nation, and earning the title given to him by an admirer, of the best lobbyist in the country, by his indefatigable and unofficial labors with timid politicians and halting legislators. Mobs were trying in vain, in obedience to the demands of slavery, to put a stop to free speech in the North, as they had already put a stop to it in the South, where free speech, free press, free schools, and free labor were catalogued together in a common denunciation. The great Evangelical Societies—preëminently the American Board

and the American Tract Society — were
silent before slavery, if not acquiescent in
it, because all Evangelical Christians did not
agree in condemning it. The American
Missionary Association had just been organized in Albany on a platform of freedom to
speak the truth and the whole truth in
preaching the Gospel.

The first sermon of the young preacher
was published in full in the *New York
Tribune,*—a more rare compliment in those
days than in ours. It was on the text
" Every man shall give account of *himself*
unto God." In the sermon as read to-day
there is nothing extraordinary except its
cumulative proofs from life in support of the
text. But in its recognition of human
liberty and human responsibility it at once
identified the young preacher as belonging
theologically to the New Puritanism. His
second notable sermon was the fourth one
preached in Brooklyn, on the evening of
October 10, the first Sunday after his
coming to the church. It was a call to arms

against intemperance and slavery, especially
the latter. It identified him, not only with
the New Puritanism, but with the radical
wing of the New Puritanism, for in it he
identified social morality with personal and
spiritual religion. The church was organized with but twenty-one members. But it
rapidly drew to itself men and women
attracted by the courage even more than by
the eloquence of the preacher, sharing his
convictions and eager to share in his work.
So rapid and so substantial was the growth
of the church that when, a little over two
years later (January 13, 1849), the building
was destroyed by fire, the church was strong
enough in both courage and money to buy
additional land, in order to enlarge its
accommodations and erect the structure in
which it has ever since worshiped. It is
not my purpose to trace the subsequent
history of Mr. Beecher or of Plymouth
Church. This has been often done and is
in print, easily accessible to any reader. I
propose on this background of history,

rapidly and imperfectly etched, to try to tell you for what, during forty years, the church and its pastor stood, and for what the church and its present pastor still stand.

In the first place, Mr. Beecher, from the very beginning, was a preacher of Christ, and this church has been from the very beginning a Christian church. There are two ways in which men may come to Christ: one through acquaintance with him as a man—as Peter and James and John came; and the other through a vision of him as a God—as Paul came. Henry Ward Beecher came to Jesus Christ through a vision of him as God. Let me read his account of his experience:

"I was a child of teaching and prayer; I was reared in the household of faith; I knew the Catechism as it was taught; I was instructed in the Scriptures as they were expounded from the pulpit, and read by men : and yet, till after I was twenty-one years old, I groped without the knowledge of God in Christ Jesus. I know not what the tablets of eternity have written down, but I think that when I stand in Zion and before God, the brightest thing which I shall look back upon will be that blessed morning of May when it pleased God to reveal to my wandering soul the idea that it was his nature to love a man in his sins for the sake of helping him out of them; that he did not do it out of compliment to Christ, or to a law, or a plan of salvation, but from the fullness of his great heart; that he was a Being not made mad by sin, but sorry; that he was not furious with wrath toward the sinner, but pitied him—in short, that he felt toward me as my mother felt toward me, to whose eyes my wrong-doing brought tears, who never pressed me so close to her as when I had done wrong, and who would fain, with her yearning love, lift me out of trouble. And when I found that Jesus Christ had such a disposition, and that when his disciples did wrong, he drew them closer to him than he did before ; and when pride and jealousy, and rivalry, and all vulgar and worldly feelings rankled in their bosoms, he opened his heart to them as a medicine to heal these infirmities;—when I found that it was Christ's nature to lift men out of weakness to strength, out of impurity to goodness, out of everything low and debasing to superiority, I felt that I had found a God.

"I shall never forget the feelings with which I walked forth that May morning. The golden pavements will never feel to my feet as then the grass felt to them; and the singing of the birds in the woods—for I roamed in the woods—was cacophonous to the sweet music of my thoughts, and there were no forms in the universe which seemed to me graceful enough to represent the Being the conception of whose character had just dawned upon my mind. I felt, when I had, with the Psalmist, called upon the heavens, the earth, the mountains, the streams, the floods, the birds, the beasts, and universal being, to praise God, that I had called upon nothing that could praise him enough for the revelation of such a nature as that in the Lord Jesus Christ."

Our knowledge comes from our experience. Calvin, as a student in Paris, was called the Accuser, because he was so rigorous in his conscience against himself and against every one else. Luther found his message when it was whispered to his own heart, The just shall live by faith; and in it he found peace. And when the message of God in Christ was proclaimed to Mr. Beecher's heart, the message was given to him which all the rest of his life he proclaimed. He was not primarily a preacher of righteousness, not primarily an anti-slavery preacher, not primarily a preacher of law or doctrine or theology of any kind;

he was primarily a preacher of Christ. The
one great book of his life, written as a book,
not composed of spoken words reported,
was the *Life of Jesus, the Christ ;* and when
that Life was left unfinished, because his
life had been broken in upon, and his sons
undertook to finish it for him, they found
in his sermons enough of description of
Christ's life to complete the work, with one
single great exception. He had never ven-
tured to describe the passion and death of
Christ upon the cross, because he could not
command himself to do it.

At one time Mr. Beecher lectured in a
" Fraternity Course," projected by the
young men of Theodore Parker's church for
charitable purposes. The Course included
Mr. Parker, together with six or eight of the
other best known lyceum orators of that
day ; but men who forgot that Paul preached
to Jews and to pagans set their batteries
in array against Henry Ward Beecher for
lecturing to radical Unitarians. In his
answer he said this (I read it not as an

accurate definition of his theology, I do not think it is, but as an exposition of his own personal experience): " Men at large will be apt to say that I have done a more exemplary Christian act, in daring to avow an *ethical* sympathy with Theodore Parker, between whom and myself there exists an irreconcilable theological difference, than if I had bombarded him for a whole year and refused to take his hand. . . . Could Theodore Parker worship my God ? Christ Jesus is his name. All that there is of God to me is bound up in that name. A dim and shadowy effluence rises from Christ, and that I am taught to call the Father. A yet more tenuous and invisible film of thought arises, and that is the Holy Spirit. But neither is to me aught tangible, restful, accessible."

This Apostolic conception of Christ as the one Image of the invisible God, to be worshiped and glorified, together with the Father and the Holy Spirit, Mr. Beecher never lost. It was his conception, and urderlay his religious life and his pulpit teaching, to the end of his life. In 1886, one year before his death, this is what he said to the ministers in London:

"Now, if you ask me if I believe in the divinity of Christ,—I do not believe in anything else. Let a man stand and look at the sun, then ask him what he sees besides. Nothing; it blinds him. There is nothing else to me when I am thinking of God; it fills the whole sphere, the heaven of heavens, the whole earth and all time; and out of that boundlessness of love and out of that infiniteness of divine faculty and capacity it seems to me that he is, to my thought, what summer is when I see it marching on after the cold winter is over. I know where the light comes from and I know where the warmth comes from. When I see anything going on for good and for the staying of evil I know it is the Sun of Righteousness, and the name to me is Jesus—every time Jesus. For him I live, for him I love, for him I labor, for him I rejoice in my remaining strength, for him I thank God that I have yet so much in me that can spend and be spent for the only one great cause which should lift itself above every other cause in this whole world."

You will bear me witness that I do not often speak of denominations by name, and it is a habit of mine not to use theological terminology, but I confess it fills me with wonder that Mr. Beecher should ever have been regarded as a Unitarian, or this church should ever have been looked at as in any sense a Unitarian church, or, if I may be allowed to say so, that its present pastor should ever have been thought to be Unitarian in his tendency. That there are certain great truths which Channing proclaimed, and which Mr. Beecher held, I do perfectly believe; and I am glad to take truth wherever I can find it. If I can find it in a Roman Catholic bishop, in a Unitarian teacher, in a Friends' conventicle— wherever I can find truth, I will take it. But the heart of Mr. Beecher's teaching was this: that Jesus Christ was God manifest in the flesh. The center that holds this church together is its faith in Jesus Christ and its loyalty to him. And what Mr. Beecher held and this church holds on this subject, I hold no less earnestly. We do not ask what men believe on other things,

what they think about decrees or fore-
ordination. I think we would even let a
man join us who believes in limited atone-
ment and special election; he might be as
heretical as the old-time Puritans, and we
would not close the door on him. The one
thing we demand is loyalty to Jesus Christ.
Some of us believe in infant baptism, and
some do not; some believe in universal salvation, some in conditional immortality, and
some in endless punishment; some are
liberal and progressive, and some are conservative: we do not ask what they think on
these questions. The one thing that holds
us together is this: we all love Christ as
our Saviour; we all acknowledge him as our
Master; we all follow him as our Leader;
we all bow down to him with absolute
allegiance as our Lord. I will exercise my
own rational judgment in determining what
he said; I will exercise it on the Gospels as
freely as I exercise it anywhere else; for God
gave us our reason to use. But when I have
found out what Christ teaches, that is final,

that to me is truth: and when I find out what Christ commands, that is final, that to me is law: and when I find out where Christ leads, that is final; that is where I mean to follow, God helping me. First of all, the foundation of all, the most important of all, this church is in its very heart, as Mr. Beecher was in his heart, and as I hope before God I am in my heart, a loyal subject of Jesus Christ.

Rooted in this faith in Christ was that great faith of his, of which he was preëminently a herald—God is love. If I might specify the three characteristics of what I call the New Puritanism, they would be these: first, man is free; secondly, in all sane men is the light that lighteth every man that cometh into the world; thirdly, God is love. Finney was the exponent of the first: his message was the law of liberty. Bushnell was the exponent of the second: his message was that in the light within men is the life of men. Mr. Beecher was the exponent of the third: God

is love. Because he believed that God is
love, he believed in an emotional and an
enthusiastic religion. One of his earliest
sermons was a plea for enthusiasm; and in
that time the church did not believe in
enthusiasm. The measures which Dr. Kirk
was using in Albany, which Dr. Finney was
using all over the country, which Dr.
Lyman Beecher had used in the West, were
called new measures. To ask a man to rise
in church for prayer, to ask him to acknowledge Christ before men, to ask him then
and there to give his heart to God,—these
were new measures. Mr. Beecher believed
in them, and used them. He believed in
revivals of religion and labored in them.
This church believed in revivals of religion;
I hope it believes in such revivals of religion
now. It was born in a revival; it has been
nurtured in revivals; it has carried the
spirit of revival with it ever since. It is
true, the methods and the measures have
changed; but it is not true that the spirit
has changed.

And because Mr. Beecher believed and
because we believe in love as the heart of
God, therefore he believed and we believe
in a natural religion—for is it not natural
for people to love ? Is the mother who
does not care for her child a natural
mother or an unnatural mother ? Is the
man who does not care for his country a
natural man or an unnatural man ? Is the
friend who feels no friendship for the companion at his side a natural man or an
unnatural man ? If religion is love, then
religion is natural. We are accused of
decrying supernatural religion. If by that
is meant that we affirm that religion, in the
heart and essence of it and in all the phases
of it, is most natural, then I plead guilty to
the charge. We believe that religion is the
natural life of a right soul, and that to live
apart from God is against nature, contrary
to nature, unnatural. And so we believe,
and he believed, in a rational religion—in
the application of the whole man to religion,
and the use of the whole man in the relig-

ious life. We believe that religion does not stifle the reason and bid men refuse to use it; we believe that religion incites men to a larger and freer use of the reason. The Christian minister should be the freest of all free-thinkers.

For the same reason we believe in a vital religion, a religion of the common life. The old definition between the secular and the religious we repudiate. I learned this lesson in my youth, in Plymouth Church. I was getting up a concert for the Young Men's Christian Association; it was to be held here in Plymouth Church; I wrote out a notice for Mr. Beecher to read: "There will be," said the notice, "some secular music and some sacred music." He read it, and then commented thus: "All good music is sacred, and all bad music is execrably secular." Religion might be not inaptly defined, the art of living. I will not say right living, because no living is living that is not right living. Wrong living is death, not life. Religion is the life of the conscience, of the faith, of the hope, of the love, of the reverence; it is the life of the eyes, of the fingers, of the feet, of the whole man. It is to be carried out in the factory, in the store, in the office, in society, in the home, in all the places of life,— and therefore in the intellect. The notion that there are two departments of man, one religious and the other secular, that the goats live in the secular and the sheep live in the religious, is all based on a misinterpretation of one of Paul's declarations— " The natural man receiveth not the things of the spirit of God; . . . neither can he know them." What he means is this: The "natural man "—that is, the mere animal man—cannot understand the supernatural, supersensuous world. To understand that world we must rise above the animal condition and enter into a higher realm, the spiritual. But that realm is open to every man. Whosoever will, may take of the water of life freely.

I wish I could make you see how natural

a thing it is to love God as God loves you, and how unnatural a thing it is not to do it; how natural a thing it is to pray, giving thanks for his goodness, and how unnatural a thing it is to live with closed lips; how natural a thing it is to take the inspiration of his love and carry it out in daily life and service to others, and how unnatural a thing it is to live a selfish, worldly, mean, and despicable life. There is not one of you who has not wings, and the air is all about you. You cannot fly without air; no! But God has surrounded the world with air, and he has given you the wings—now rise and fly. Do not be a grub; that is the unnatural thing.

And because God is love, and religion is love, and life is love, and love is natural to man, religion is to be seen in carrying love out in daily conduct. There is no religion which is not ethical. There is no religion in the emotions excited and life left impoverished. There is no religion in ecstatic prayers and mean and niggardly living,—

to quote Mr. Beecher again, "We cannot pray cream and live skim-milk." From the first that has been the message of this pulpit. Because we have loved Christ, and because we have loved the God whom Christ has revealed to us, and because we have loved our fellow men in that they are God's children and are revealed to us in Christ, therefore have we stood against whatever dwarfs and diminishes and belittles humanity, therefore have we stood for whatever ennobles, enfranchises, and lifts humanity up. Would that you younger men and women could see in what condition was society in America when the American Tract Society and the American Board and the American Home Missionary Society were all silent on the subject of slavery, because all Evangelical Christians were not agreed upon the subject of slavery; when the great Methodist Church and the great Presbyterian Church were divided, one of them almost wholly, and the other partly, on the question of slavery; what it was

when, if a man spoke for freedom in New
York or Philadelphia or Boston, he did so
at the hazard of violence from a mob, and
perhaps at the hazard of his life; what it
was when men were vilifying Sumner and
Chase and Garrison and Phillips, and even
John G. Whittier, because they had raised
a voice for the freedom of the slave; what
it was, in a new church enterprise in this
great commercial metropolis, to proclaim
liberty unto all God's children; and then
what it was for the merchants, the lawyers,
the business men, whose business prosperity
apparently depended on silent lips, to rally
around that new herald and say, Go on,
speak for us, and we will stand by you!
It is easy now. It does not now require
bravery to be brave in Plymouth pulpit.
He who stands here can speak on the labor
question, on Biblical criticism, on theological and ethical problems, on any phase
of any theological or ethical problem, and
the church, whether it agrees with him or
not, will say, Speak, if you speak your own

convictions. The one thing this church would not endure would be this: that its minister should be afraid to say what he thought was the truth. It does not take courage to speak freely on this platform. A man would have to be a hero in cowardice to be a coward here.

I have tried to indicate the features of the Old Puritanism—a fatalistic system, with God as sovereign Judge; and the features of the New Puritanism—man a free moral agent, with God the all-loving Father: and now I put them side by side and ask you not only to judge them as they look, but to judge them by their fruits. We have had the experience of something like one hundred years of the New Puritanism, beginning in 1800, growing stronger and stronger, until it came to its flower about the middle of this century; and what is the fruition? Intemperance still exists. Yes, but not in the church of Christ. We are not all total abstainers, and we are not all of us prohibitionists; but the church does stand for self-control, and against the traffic that makes money out of the death of men. We have seen slavery abolished and every chain broken, and the men who broke the chains—I repeat it—were the same men who were preaching the New Puritanism. It would be difficult to find a single abolitionist belonging to the Old Puritanism. We have seen foreign and home missions both born. Then, not a church with a mission chapel—now, no church of size in any of our cities without one; then, no foreign missionary organization, no home missionary organization — now, a foreign missionary organization carrying the gospel to the heathen, and a home missionary organization building up the waste places of our own country, and the American Missionary Association working among the poor and the outcast, where no man was allowed to work in 1850. And all this having its fountain and its source in spiritual life.

I do not know whether I ought to speak of this church or not. God knows I do not

wish to praise or to flatter, certainly not to
apologize or excuse; and yet, when we are
told that the New Puritanism is undermin-
ing life and destroying faith, I have a right
to point to the fifty years of history of this
Christian church. Still it ministers every
Sunday to two essentially distinct large congregations. Still its voice is carried beyond
its walls to unseen and unnumbered auditors
beyond. Still through its ministry men and
women are brought to confess their faith in
God and in his Son Jesus Christ. In fifty
years, three thousand six hundred and
thirty-three have thus come into the kingdom of God through the doors of this
church.[1] The love of Christ draws men
who could not be coerced by fear. What
sort of Christians does the New Puritanism
make? Probably not unlike other Christians
—some good, some indifferent, some poor.
Yet in answer to that question I may point

---

[1] An average of a little over seventy-two a year.
During the ten years since Mr. Beecher's death, six
hundred have joined the church, an average of sixty a
year, without special measures or meetings of any kind.

to the fact that in our three Sunday-schools are gathered every Sunday an average of over twelve hundred, studying the Bible; that we do not lack faithful teachers, that on this fiftieth anniversary-day every class is supplied, and we have a waiting-list of volunteers to call from in the future; that Plymouth Church is a week-day as well as a Sunday church; that with its two Kindergartens, its two Sewing-schools, its two Societies of Christian Endeavor, its three Boys' Clubs, its Boys' Brigade, its Mothers' Meetings, and its Missionary Societies, there is rarely an evening in the week in which there are not going on contemporaneously two or more meetings for the service of God in and through the service of humanity; and that an average of ten to twelve thousand dollars is given annually, all of it spontaneously, most of it in modest contributions—aside from the expenses of the church itself—for the support of this work of Christ by Christ's disciples in this church of Christ.

The church has had its trials. Its home burnt down, that is built again; attacked and vilified in the person of its pastor for his heresies and erraticisms, it has maintained itself unscathed; assaulted in the very citadel of its life, the only effect has been to rally its members around about its leader and make it more united and more stalwart than before. Suddenly in the midst of the battle the flag is seen to waver and the flag-bearer falls in death; but the church halts only for a moment, then gathers around that flag stronger than ever, better organized, to go on following another standard-bearer. For it has not been the flag-bearer, it has been the flag, and yet more the Christ whom that flag means, that has held this church together, and will hold it together so long as God has work for it to do. And, please God, with our face to the future, following him, we will go on, preaching the freedom of man's will, preaching the religion of righteousness and practical love, preaching the Christ of God as the revelation of his infinite and all-saving mercy, not fearing lest we go too far, for we have not yet overtaken Christ, not fearing lest we be led astray,—no fear of that so long as we follow where he leads the way:—first, last, and all the time, a church of Jesus Christ.

Puritan Principles and the Modern World.

AMORY H. BRADFORD.

II.

Puritan Principles and the Modern World.[1]

By AMORY H. BRADFORD, D.D.,
Of First Congregational Church, Montclair, N. J.

"I proclaimed a fast there at the river Ahava, that we might afflict ourselves before our God to seek of him the right way."—*Ezra*, viii. 21.

THE sleepy river flows as slowly by Delfshaven to-day as when two hundred and seventy-seven years ago a little company of English Christians embarked on its waters, for the most memorable voyage ever sailed on any sea.

The precise point of their departure cannot be identified. The river is lined with warehouses and factories, and neither tradi-

[1] Plymouth Church, Sunday evening, May 17, 1897.

77

tion nor history speaks of the exact spot
where the *Speedwell* was anchored. But
some things which preceded the embarka-
tion are known, and among them that a day
of fasting and prayer was observed, when
John Robinson, with the inspiration of a
prophet and the tenderness of a pastor,
preached from the text which has been
chosen for our text to-day. The solemnity
of the occasion cannot be reproduced. It
was one of those historic moments when
men chosen of God dimly realize that they
are facing a mission of vast and mysterious
magnitude, and therefore humble themselves before Almighty God and seek to
know his will. At least one sentence in
that sermon has become immortal. Indeed
it may be questioned if any other sentiment ever spoken by any English preacher
is so vividly remembered or will live so
long. Edward Winslow, writing twenty
years after, in speaking of Robinson and his
sermon, says: " Amongst other wholesome
instructions and exhortations he used these

expressions, or to the same purpose." (I quote but one:) "And if God should reveal anything to us by any other instrument of his, to be as ready to receive it as ever we were to receive any truth by his ministry. For he was very confident the Lord had more truth and light yet to break forth out of his holy Word."

The Pilgrim Fathers were all Puritans, and yet they were not bigots. Their eyes were open toward the future, but they did not forget the truths which had been forged in the fires of the Reformation. The sermon of John Robinson on that memorable day was an eloquent and solemn presentation of the principles of Puritanism; the principles which in England led to Hampden, Harry Vane, Cromwell, the Puritan Revolution; the principles which inspired the heroic souls who dared a winter voyage on the North Atlantic in a craft smaller than ocean yachts to-day; which led to the compact in the cabin of the *Mayflower*, to the Declaration of Independence, to the

Union of States, and to all that distinguishes what is best in American civilization. Therefore it has seemed as if this sermon and this text were the proper starting-point for a consideration of the " Relation of Puritan Principles to the Modern World."

No people can ever safely forget or neglect the source of their loftiest inspirations. We shall appreciate our destiny only as we first appreciate our beginnings. The roots of the American Republic are bedded deeply in the soil of Puritanism. Were some of our ancestors Scotch ? They were Scotch Puritans. Were others Dutch? They came here with the principles which so powerfully influenced the Pilgrims in Holland. Were still others English? In so far as their work was vital and enduring they were men of the same spirit and temper as those who a little later in England fought at Marston Moor and Naseby, Worcester and Dunbar. Others may sneer at Puritanism, but for an American to do so is like a son desecrating the home in which he was born and the memory of the parents by whom he was trained.

What were the distinctive Principles of Puritanism? They were the following:

Every individual has immediate access to God, and in all the affairs of the spirit is responsible to him alone.

As men are responsible to God alone, all are under a sacred obligation to insist on the right and duty of absolute mental freedom, unhindered by dictation from any human authority.

The true church of Christ is composed of all regenerate persons, and all are to be regarded as regenerate who prove their faith by holy character.

As a later though perfectly logical and necessary result of what precedes: all believers have equal rights before God, and when they act together the body of believers may be trusted.

These principles may seem somewhat abstract and academic, but they made the Puritan Revolution in Great Britain a neces-

sity and the American Republic a possibility. Locked in their somewhat rough
exterior is the life which thrills in modern
liberty, and they suggest with clearness the
social state which will prevail when the
noblest religious, social, and political ideals
have had time to work to their legitimate
ends.

What was the Genesis of Puritanism?

It is difficult to find the source of any
river. Rivulets run to a thousand valleys,
and the spring in which the most remote
seems to have its birth may have unseen
streams reaching to far-distant fountains.
The source of every river is in the clouds;
their source is the ocean, and the ocean is a
fountain because of the attraction of the
sun. There have been Puritans in all ages
and among all religions. Moses was a
Puritan; so were the prophets; so were the
apostles; so were Augustine and Marsiglio,
so were Luther and Calvin. The Puritans
have always been those who have insisted

that spirit is more than form, and that character is more than ceremony. The noblest utterance of Hebrew Puritanism was this: " What doth the Lord require of thee, but to do justly, to love mercy, and to walk humbly before thy God?"

Historically, Puritanism as we understand it began soon after the Church in England under Henry the Eighth was separated from the Church in Rome. The cause of that separation was vicious. A lecherous king wished freedom from Papal dictation in order that he might be divorced and thus be able lawfully to marry again. After the division the Church of England remained the same as before, except that the King was in the place of the Pope. The separation was called a reformation. From the beginning, however, men of lofty character insisted that it had not gone far enough; that the Church should not only be separated from Papal dictation, but from all those tenets and practices which were hostile to righteousness. From that time there

were Puritans in name as well as in fact,
and they were a constantly growing force in
the ecclesiastical and political life of Great
Britain. They insisted on purity of character as essential to service in Church and
State. All were not Separatists then, as
they are not now. There are Puritans in the
Church of England to-day, as there were
then. The Presbyterians of Scotland were
as distinctly Puritans as the Separatists of
England. Puritanism was a spirit which
manifested itself in many forms. When
the Separatists under Cromwell defeated
the Presbyterians under Lesly at Dunbar,
the fight was between the Puritan who
believed in a State Church and the Puritan
who believed that union of Church and
State was a device of the devil. Puritan
principles are not limited to any ecclesiastical organizations. They came to this country with the Scotch-Irish, with the Pilgrims
of Plymouth, and the Puritans of Massa-
chusetts Bay. They are making themselves
felt now as clearly as two centuries ago.

The Nonconformist Conscience in England is a new manifestation of Puritanism; the municipal revival in the United States is another. Both are the insistence that the offices of the State are as holy as those of the Church, and that no man ought to represent the State in any official position who is not pure in his character and unselfish in his aspirations and methods.

From the first, Puritanism has been distinctly a religious movement, but it quickly ceased to be ecclesiastical. It is as religious to-day as when the Pilgrims sailed or Cromwell fought or Milton sang; and it is religious now, as then, because a true view of religion embraces all which concerns the welfare of man both in time and eternity. Puritanism stands for reality; for character; for clean living as a condition of public service; for recognition of responsibility to God; for the supremacy of the spirit. When Oliver Cromwell entered Parliament in 1653, and said, pointing to one member, "There sits a taker of bribes;" to another, "There sits a man whose religion is a farce;" to another, using the hardest name possible, which I soften, " There sits a man whose personal conduct is impure and foul;" and then in the name of Almighty God broke up the Parliament, he was the impersonation of Puritanism; and for one, I wish he would rise from his grave and in the same spirit enter some of our halls of legislation, both state and national.

So much for the genesis of Puritanism.

What has been the Effect of Puritanism on the World?

To ask that question is to answer it. It fought the priesthood in the Hebrew times, and insisted on genuineness and spirituality. It was personified in John Calvin when he wrought to perfect expression the truth that every individual may come into the immediate presence of God and is responsible to him alone. It inspired the Puritan Revolution. It sent the Pilgrims to Plymouth. It made this nation a republic, and has dominated the whole British Empire, so that the Union Jack stands for a liberty quite as ample as that represented by the Stars and Stripes.

At one time Puritanism seemed synonymous with narrow theology, bigotry, witchburning, sanctimoniousness, spiritual despotism. That was because its principles had not had time to work into life and institutions. Freedom of thought is now realized wherever Puritanism is in control. The fact that men are responsible to God alone, and therefore that no earthly sovereign has any divine right, has undermined or limited every throne in Europe. Puritanism compelled the modern movement in theology, and John Calvin and Jonathan Edwards were its greatest prophets and the lineal theological ancestors of Horace Bushnell, Henry Ward Beecher, and Phillips Brooks. Puritanism has always insisted on a high standard of character as a prerequisite to public service; that no man should be in the Church whose life has not experienced a change so vital as to be called a new birth; that the State is as holy as the Church, and therefore that those who minister at its altars should be without taint. Puritanism is a spirit, but a spirit which has always found expression in men and institutions—and what men and institutions have sprung into being at its touch! There were all the heroes of the Puritan Revolution in England—Hampden, Pym, Sir Harry Vane, John Howe and John Owen, Milton, the seer and prophet as well as the poet of the Commonwealth, and Cromwell, the kingliest soul that ever ruled Great Britain. In later days there have been such men as Bright in Parliament, Gordon in the field, Dale, Maclaren, and Spurgeon in the pulpit, and Robert Browning among the poets. The history of America in large part is either the history of Puritanism, or of those who were made great by its ideals. Ideally this Republic rests on these four corner-stones: the right and privilege of the individual to come into the immediate presence of God; absolute freedom in all matters of religion; righteousness of character essential to public service; and, the universal brotherhood of man. These truths have commanded the loyalty of the best men in our churches; they have inspired our noblest preachers; they thrill in the music of poets like Lowell, Whittier, Longfellow; they are recognized by so many of our politicians as have learned that the State was made for man and not man for the State. The most beneficent and enduring elements in the political, social, literary, religious life of the world for two hundred years either has been the expression of the Puritan spirit or from it has received inspiration. And this leads now to a more important inquiry.

Is there any Serious Demand in the Modern World for that which is Essential in the Principles of Puritanism?

Before that question can be intelligently answered we must have some accurate ideas

about this modern world.   It has great ex-
cellencies; has it any serious perils? I shall
limit the field of observation to our own
country.   He who knows the dominant
forces in any one civilized nation practically
knows those of the world.   Four facts meet
every student of the history of our country
and of our time.

There is a wide-spread and growing tendency toward the effacement of the feeling
of individual responsibility to God.   The
everlasting obligation of men to choose
right, and their moral peril if they refuse,
is not as vivid as it should be.   Thomas
Carlyle said that the Puritan Revolution
was the last of the heroisms.   He was
wrong.   Heroism is the monopoly of no age
and no creed, and its source is always in the
consciousness of responsibility to God.
Cromwell refused to be king because he was
not convinced that God had called him to
wear a crown.   How many vacant chairs
there would be in the high places of government if all who have not heard a divine call

were to retire from public service! We have
Tammany politics, the defeat of Arbitration
Treaties, and juggling with municipal fran-
chises, because God has no place in the
plans of those who sit in legislative halls;
we have pagan immoralities introduced at
banquets, and pagan vice winked at in high
places, because a day in which God will
judge every man is no longer dreaded; we
have monopolies reaching out to embrace
and strangle our liberties, because greed of
gold and power has blinded men to God.

Another characteristic of our time is a
misconception of what is meant by intellectual and spiritual freedom. Liberty of
thought is the supreme achievement of
modern times. There is no longer any
human authority in the realm of religion.
Councils, assemblies, states, are all composed of fallible men. No thinking person
now accepts any doctrine in science, political economy, or religion solely because it is
hallowed by age or has been championed by
the great of other times. There is no holy

of holies in the realm of truth. The blind can see that the days of authority in all matters of thought are not only numbered but ended. But the pendulum has swung too far. Liberty of thought does not mean freedom to believe a lie; does not mean that there is no authority in truth; does not mean that it is of little importance what men believe; does not mean that one creed is as good as another. And yet this fallacy is growing in our land. It is said that one creed is as good as another,—which means there is no truth. Men are asking what they like to believe, not what they ought to believe. Freedom to think and to express thought is a condition of growth; freedom to think without the consciousness of obligation to accept truth and cling to it forever is a delusion and a peril. That was a wise word of the author of *The Way Out of Agnosticism:* "Either we must cease to think, or learn to think more profoundly."

Let us cling to our liberty, but remember that that does not mean freedom to play with sanctities,—to seek to revive mysteries which have been dead so long that no one knows when they died; but rather the duty to think, to think hard, to think long; until there shall come a glimpse of the unity in which all things cohere, or until there breaks upon the vision such a revelation as is given only to those who reverently and patiently knock at the door of truth.

A third characteristic of the modern world is a dimming of the lines which separate virtue and vice, right and wrong. This is evident most of all in current social and domestic ideals. The civilization of a nation is always according to its standard of moral purity. Those who reverence and safeguard their homes prosper and endure; those who are fascinated by immoralities sow the seed of their own decay. In these days Puritanism is sneered at in high circles as prudery, and the divorce courts are mills that never cease to grind a baleful grist.

There is yet one more characteristic of our time and our nation which it is painful to state and more painful to be compelled to recognize. We are living in a republic and compelled to witness the defeat of the people. If I were asked, What is the most ominous fact in the life of this country to-day? I should without hesitation answer, The defeat of the people. The fundamental principle of modern civilization is the right of the people to rule; but in this country at least the people do not rule. Two very simple illustrations will suffice— but they might be indefinitely multiplied.

In a small town the question is merely one of the granting of a franchise to a trolley company. The people say: "Restrict and safeguard, and let it come;" but outside monopolies, thinking only of dividends, either buy up a council, or procure special legislation and drive through their own schemes without the slightest regard to the wishes of those who own the property, whose homes are invaded, and whose life-purposes are ruined. Thus the people are defeated.

Two great nations, after glaring at each other for more than a century conclude that they have shaken fists long enough, and that they had better clasp hands and prove themselves the brothers that they are in blood, in language, in history, in religion; and the people in both nations lift such a cry of gladness as has not been heard for a quarter of a century. This is the people's business, and they have a right to be heeded. But no; the machinery of government is straightway invoked that prejudice may rule and the people be humiliated and disgraced. Thus government of the people, for the people, and by the people has failed almost before the echoes of Lincoln's oration have died away. I do not speak as a pessimist. It is not pessimism to face facts. Most of our cities are ruled by corrupt oligarchies; most of our states are in the hands of selfish politicians; and international problems, instead of being solved by representatives of the people, are shelved by those who misrepresent them.

These four facts cannot be evaded; they should be honestly and fearlessly faced: Consciousness of individual responsibility to God is dim; playing with everlasting realities is called liberty of thought; the line between right and wrong, purity and vice, is being rubbed out; and, the people are systematically and constantly defeated. This is not all there is to modern life, but these are our perils.

What does this modern world need? A revival of Puritanism. Individuals and society should rise to a comprehension of the truth that all men live in the presence of the Almighty, and are responsible to him. What made the Ironsides invincible? They could fight all day because they had prayed all night. They endured as seeing Him who is invisible. On the field of Dunbar Cromwell snatched victory from what had seemed sure defeat. When the sun rose and the enemy fled, he halted his troops and, riding before them, sang, " Let God arise; let his enemies be scattered!"

God may be realized, — that realization makes prophets and heroes. Introduce into our modern life the glad and awful reality that God besets us behind and before; that there is no space in the universe in which any man can hide from him; bring out again the fact of a judgment-seat before which all some time and somehow must stand,—and there will be less trifling with the everlasting sanctities. Those who have seen God will not dare his displeasure. This is what the modern world most needs. Preachers who experience God will have time neither for pyrotechnics nor pantomime; teachers will realize with Thomas Arnold that a life of truthfulness and genuineness is the first and most inspiring of all instruction; and legislators will enter capitals with the humility of those who have received a divine call.

As it brushes away the assumed authority of churches, councils, schools, and all other assemblies of presumptuous and fallible men, Puritanism insists that while there must be perfect freedom of thought, it should be a freedom consistent with the obligation of every man to seek and obey truth. Authority in the hands of fallible men becomes an enormity, but the authority of the truth can be evaded only at peril. Puritans believe something, and believe it with all their hearts. Like Cromwell, they protect others in *their* beliefs, while they are willing to fight and to die for their own. In these days, when the foundations of faith tremble; when the doctrines which once made heroes are being questioned; when foreign cults are coming in like a flood; when the intellectual and spiritual world is in a state of unrest, above all things there should be intellectual honesty and thoroughness; unwillingness to be satisfied with any sham, however ancient or honored; the determination to think every subject through until truth is found, wherever it may lead. These qualities always have been and always will be the very essence of Puritanism. Puritanism can be satisfied only with reality. It insists on mental freedom, and is afraid only of that which is false. The modern world asks what pleases; Puritanism asks what is right. The modern world says: Every man is at liberty to think as he chooses; Puritanism replies: Yes, so long as he remembers that no one can escape from the authority of truth.

The lines separating right and wrong, virtue and vice, are growing dim in this modern world. Luxury and effeminacy are taking their places. Literature in great part is becoming mere dirt, a covering of cancers with cloth of gold; the stage has forgotten its Greek dignity and become, largely, a place where vice panders to vice. Let the old Puritans come back once more: they must never again desecrate cathedrals or dare to destroy that which is beautiful in art; but let them with their austere moralities deal with the paganisms, the luxuries, the fashionable vices, the polluted literature, and the brazen effrontery of those who

disgrace the stage. Better the time when
a man was forbidden to kiss his wife on the
Lord's day than a land without any Lord's
day; better the abolition of the play than
plays which stimulate sensuality; better a
solemn face than one blotched with vice.
The modern world needs no distortions of
Puritanism, but its essential spirit — the
spirit which will never compromise with
evil, and which is as loyal to purity in the
individual, the family, and society as King
Arthur was loyal to his knightly vows.

The sad fact which faces all who love
their country in these days and in this
Republic is that in the land of freedom, the
land of Washington, of Lincoln and of
Grant, the people for whom the fathers died
are either defeated or in peril of defeat.
In the home of brotherhood, brotherhood is
outraged; and where the voice of the many
should be heeded it is publicly derided.
Nothing will give to the American people
the realization of their ideals but the political principle for which the Pilgrims stood;

namely, the people and the whole people acting together should always be trusted. Above every other truth Puritanism places God the Sovereign, and then declares that before that Sovereign all men have equal rights. It never asks where a man was born, what is his name, or what is the color of his skin; but insists that the whole people are to be trusted, without regard to accidents of birth or wealth. This world belongs to all the people. Their voice may not always be the voice of God, but it is nearer to it than any other sound ever heard on the earth. When the people have a chance to speak their convictions they are seldom wrong. This is the dispensation of man, not of any class; and yet classes stand in the way of man. Colleges and schools, press and pulpit, ought to unite in a crusade for the deliverance of the people from those who, masquerading in the livery of liberty, are its worst enemies.

The evils of the modern world demand that emphasis once more be strong and clear on the four truths which are the corner-stones of Puritanism:

All men are responsible to God.

All must have freedom of thought, but never liberty to believe error or to do wrong.

The line separating right and wrong is an everlasting one; it is, in the nature of things, a part of the order of the universe.

The whole people, since they have the same Father and the same King in the realm of spirit, have the same rights, spiritual, social, religious; and they can be and ought to be trusted.

The Pilgrims to whom John Robinson preached on that memorable day before the *Speedwell* sailed were Puritans. The Pilgrims who landed at Plymouth were Puritans; their children who founded here " a Church without a Bishop, and a State without a King," were Puritans. The principles which have given us our right to be called a Christian nation were derived from the Puritans; most of our colleges were founded by Puritans; our school system came from the Puritans; our ideals are all Puritan. These ideals will become realities, and the American nation worthy to possess its privileges and possibilities, only as we are loyal to the principles and the spirit which were the inspiration of our fathers. Our hope is not in Puritanism in its narrowness and with its bigotries, but in its larger spirit which reveres God and seeks his will; which owns no authority but truth; which believes in righteousness and does right, and always and everywhere trusts the people.

I have thus spoken of our perils and our needs. Of the outcome I have no doubt. There is no room for pessimism in the creed of a Christian. We may seem to have forgotten the holiest ideals, but we shall not swing entirely away from them. Through the generations one increasing purpose runs. God fulfills his plans in many ways. To a heroic service our fathers were called: a service equally important and imperative belongs to their children. Let us gird ourselves like men for our mission, and never doubt that the victory will be with those who side with God.

I have chosen this subject for this occasion because no pulpit ever more continuously, consistently, and unflinchingly represented that which is essential and enduring in Puritanism than the one in which I have the honor to stand to-night, and which has been distinguished by the incomparable ministry of the man whose first sermon in this city we are this day celebrating. Henry Ward Beecher, strange as the saying may sound in some ears, was a Puritan of the Puritans. He had no patience with the narrowness and hardness of many who bore that great name. He delighted in the beautiful, and would never have sanctioned the defacing of the cathedrals. He rejoiced in all that makes this world bright and glad, and we cannot think of him with a demure face or as discouraging innocent pleasure. But underneath all the exuberance of his nature was such a realization of God as few men have experienced, and that was the unfail-

ing source of his personality and ministry.
To him the birds sang the songs of God; the
winds echoed the music of God; the waters
reflected the beauty of God; the heavens
declared the glory of God. The secret of
his power was in his realization that he, like
a little child, could come into the very presence of the Almighty. Out of that consciousness poured his ministry like a broad,
deep river,—sometimes placid like summer
waters; sometimes dark and threatening;
sometimes rushing and turbulent, but always flowing steadily from an inexhaustible
fountain.

Because he appreciated his responsibility
to God, he insisted as few in any time have
insisted on the privilege and duty of every
man to think for himself, and he never
doubted that to all who think honestly and
bravely will some time be given the realization of God.

Because he had seen God, he preached
righteousness with a power which has never
been surpassed. His sermons thrill with
reverence for the moral order of the world.

No medieval Calvinist was more constant or terrible in his denunciations of evil; and no disciple of modern thought ever more persuasively presented the beauty of holiness.

Because he believed in God, he believed in the brotherhood of man, and that the whole people could be trusted; and with amazing eloquence he proclaimed that doctrine until the land he loved became a land without a slave.

This greatest preacher of the modern world was one of the most distinctly typical Puritans of this or any time. It is not for me to eulogize Henry Ward Beecher; he needs no eulogy, either in this church or this city; but it is a joy to be able to recall once more the truths which he loved and proclaimed, and in the faith of which he lived and died. When he passed into the silent land

> " It seemed there came, but faint,
> As from beyond the limit of the world,
> Like the last echo born of a great cry,
> Sounds, as if some fair city were one voice
> Around a king returning from his wars."

Beecher's Influence upon Religious Thought in England.

CHARLES A. BERRY.

III.

"Beecher's Influence upon Religious Thought in England." [1]

By Rev. CHARLES A. BERRY, D.D.,
Wolverhampton, England.

IN recognition of the fact that Henry Ward Beecher, beloved as the pastor of this church, was yet the property of Christendom, and by a delicate and gracious courtesy, I have been called from the shores of my fatherland, and from the home and work I love, to speak to you to-day upon the influence of Henry Ward Beecher on teaching and preaching in Great Britain. But before proceeding to that task, not less grateful because difficult, it is my duty, as it is my privilege and my joy, to express to

---

[1] Plymouth Church, Sunday morning, Nov. 7, 1897.

the pastor, the officers, the members of this famous and influential church, the congratulations and the good wishes of a host of sister churches across the Atlantic waves. My own church especially, which has more than once come into close and sacred relations with Plymouth, and never into relations more co-operative or effective than when, during a recent and regrettable crisis, we exchanged cablegrams of mutual petition for the preservation of peace and the restoration of good will between America and England, has charged me to express to you the warmest sentiments of appreciation and regard, and most cordial prayers for your enlarged usefulness and prosperity in the new half-century on which you have entered this year. The welfare of Plymouth is indeed the solicitude of all English-speaking Christendom, not merely because of recognized debt to the ministries and achievements of a glorious past, but because of sincere desire to have those ministries attested and confirmed in a solid, sober, unbroken, and apostolical succession of saintly and serviceable fellowship. The severest, and therefore the truest, test, whether of a pastorate or of a church, and especially where great publicity and popularity have attended their union, is reached only when the two are sundered—when, on one hand, the contagious and constraining vitalities of a great personality are withdrawn, and, on the other hand, the responsive enthusiasms of an appreciative people are denied the magnetic excitation of thrilling voice, and kindling eye, and gold-tipped winged eloquence, and are driven back for their awakenment and sustenance upon the quieter but more reliable agencies of intellectual and spiritual understanding. Then it is that the secret comes out whether or not pastor and people have been walking in a vain show; whether or not, in his attraction of great multitudes, the pastor has neglected the training and the discipline of a living church; whether or not the people, seemingly so zealous for God and humanity, are the dupes of a sensuous spell, the victims of mere ravishing oratory, or the intelligent and devoted disciples and servants of a beautiful gospel, made credible by the genius of a heaven-sent interpreter. And it is from that point of view, if I may venture so to express it here this morning, that the friends of Plymouth Church in Britain discover their deepest satisfaction and joy.

Ten years have passed, and well-nigh eleven, since he was taken whose name will forever be entwined with some of your greatest national achievements and most of your ecclesiastical and theological progress. And what do we see around us to-day ? A living church—large, compact, earnest, reverent, devoted, as rich in organization as it is in life, still occupying its place down here right in the midst of this thronged and crowded city, a center of one of the most gifted and devoted Christian bands to be found anywhere in the world, a church laden with holiest traditions and memories, and

yet alive and devoted to the thought and
duty of to-day. *This* is the true Beecher
memorial, not that brass medallion (speaking as is the likeness, it suggests more than
it contains); not yon bronze statue, erected
by the love and reverence of grateful citizens; not any printed or spoken eulogy, apt
to become exaggerated, or, in fear of ex-
aggeration, to fail in tribute; but this living
church, surviving him, pulsating by his
spirit, reproducing his ideas and ideals—
this living church, that loved and loves
him so well as to turn from mere grief or
reminiscence to active service—this is his
memorial. And we across the water thank
God that his memorial is in the form of a
living fellowship rather than of cold marble
or printed eulogy.

And what is thus the best memorial to
the man who is gone is the best tribute to
the church that remains, and to him who
reluctantly, nervously, in spite of feelings
that his work lay in other directions, took
up the leadership of this church, and has

maintained, as he still maintains it, in efficiency of Christian instruction and Christian service.

Our congratulations to-day from across the water are deep and sincere. We rejoice with you over your great and glorious past. We enter, if with surprise yet with the more grateful joy, into your loving and fruitful present. We join hands with you in petitioning that, as in the past and in the present, so in days to come, you may enjoy the conscious presence of the Master, and work effectively by the grace and power of the Holy Ghost.

Now, from what I have said, it will be quite clear to you that this memorial service, at least as far as I am concerned, is neither to be an exhibition of vain and reminiscent regret, nor a mere ebullition of foolish and degrading idolatry. If to-day we look back, it is to relearn the lessons, to catch the inspirations, which sprang from the lips and the mind of your great preacher. If to-day, in looking back, we concentrate our thoughts upon a man, it is not that we may glorify him or raise him to false eminence in the thought and affection of Christendom, but that we may glorify God in him—the God who made, the God who inspired him. There is, as we all know, a false hero-worship, the worship of a man which hides God, and which the more shrivels the heart because playing upon it the fiction of enlargement. But there is a hero-worship that is true, that is divine, that is enlarging and sweetening. A great man is God's best gift to men. Not to recognize and not to cherish him is to blaspheme the bounty and the grace of God. It were, indeed, as easy to blot out from a landscape the mountain that rears its snowy crest beyond the clouds, as to forget or to ignore the presence of great personalities in God's earth and in Christ's church.

That doctrine of equality which declares that one man is as good as another is a lie. Equality of privilege, equality of opportunity, equality as sinners before God, equality as rightful claimants upon God for saving grace—that is the true equality. But in God's world, some are made to lead and some to follow, some to teach and some to learn; and any driveling doctrine of equality which would erect the lowest, the meanest, the least capable into line with the foremost, has written upon it the absolute rejection of God. His great men he sends to be brothers and to be servants; but their brotherhood and their service are constituted in this, that they must teach, that they must be obeyed, that they must lead, that they must be followed. God has gifted them with such amplitude as to live in them for the example and guidance of mankind. And hence it is that in the New Testament we never can get away from the personality of St. Paul. Modest as he was, conscious of his ill-desert in presence of the Eternal, knowing as none other could know the limitations and debilities of his own soul, yet was he conscious that God had put grace into him, and gifts such as

constituted him servant and leader of all.
And throughout his epistles we find that,
with delicacy but with unmistakable meaning, he puts his own case to the front, that
men might think, not of him, but of the
grace of God that made him; not of his
eloquence, not of his fame, not of his personality, but of the wondrous power and
the redemptive efficiency of the love of
Jesus Christ.

And so we think to-day of Henry Ward
Beecher. You cannot shut out his personality. Why should you try? By so
much as that personality made the world
brighter, God's thought clearer, man's duty
simpler, life's sufferings easier to be borne,
in that measure he was a fresh incarnation
of the Eternal Love. For that reason
we glorify God in him, and we pray that
the succession, the true apostolic and saintly succession, of God's great and gifted
ones may never cease until this weary world
has passed through all the phases of its
travail and its discipline, and is merged in

the shadowless light and the ineffable love
of God.

But now from these general remarks I
turn to my more specific subject. I am not
to speak of Beecher in the entirety of his
life—which is as merciful for me as for you;
for, if I began to get beyond the fringe of
that great personality, you would not get
dismissal until sunrise to-morrow, and then
I should not have passed the first head of
the discourse. I am to speak of Beecher's
influence on the thought and preaching of
England. That assumes that Beecher had
an influence upon the thought and preaching of England; and I am here to-day to
affirm that he had a distinct and effective
influence in those great departments of life.
Now, put that fact into juxtaposition with
another fact, which helps to interpret it and
to fix its true value. Henry Ward Beecher
was seldom seen and seldom heard by the
great masses of the people in my country.
Only a fraction of the religious leaders and
teachers of Britain ever saw that face which

reflected so much of the sunniness of God. It will appear to you quite clear, then, that his influence was not the influence of personal presence, of captivating eloquence, but was the influence of thought when reduced to the cold and lifeless level of a printed page. That fact is of value in determining the quality of Henry Ward Beecher's ministry.

There is a foolish idea in many quarters that the orator and the thinker can never be one and the same man; that the orator is a man devoted to the tricks of speech, dependent for his power upon the resourcefulness of a contagious personality; and that the thinker, on the other hand, is a man who necessarily must withdraw himself from all the activities of the world, and from the influence of great public assemblies. Never was greater mistake made in the estimate of function and faculty. There can be rhetoric without thought, but never oratory. For what is the orator? The orator is, what the word that signifies him etymologically suggests, the man who beseeches, the man who reasons, the man who pleads, the man who wins. He is the petitioner, the prophet. And what is the prophet? The man who speaks for God to men in winsome speech—speech that interprets the Eternal—and so interprets him that men want to rush after him and to embrace him. The prophet is the poet and the orator. The rhetorician, the man of words—reduce him to a printed page, and you kill both him and his speech. Beecher was a thinker gifted of God with fine faculty of vision; he saw into the deep things of God, and what he saw, God gave him tongue and lip to speak. And so his oratory was lifted far above the wind and bluster of the rhetorician, and became the fine vehicle of thoughts that burn, emotions that kindle, and reasons that bend the will and inspire the soul.

But when we turn to ask what, in this realm of thought, was Beecher's contribution to modern Christendom, we confront a task less easy; for during the period of Henry

Ward Beecher's life we in England at least, and you in America, I dare say, came under the sweep and influence of a whole host of new thinkers and new workers. I will speak of the land I know.

In England, during these fifty years past, we have seen the rise of Colenso and Biblical criticism; and, young as I am, I am old enough to remember the virulent and contemptuous abuse heaped upon the head of Bishop Colenso for his daring pioneer work in the task of rightly understanding the Scriptures of God. But his name and presence have been influential these fifty years in guiding the thought and method of Christian teachers. During the same period, at the very opposite extreme, one sees John Henry Newman and the Oxford Movement leading men away from all inquiry and from all research into absolute surrender to ecclesiastical, not to say Papal, authority. Right in the midst of this same generation rises a figure, refined, modest, little seen while yet the

figure lived, much loved since the man
within the figure passed up into the eternal. Frederick William Robertson, of
Brighton, has been in England perhaps
the most widely potent religious force of
the Victorian era, introducing preachers to
a method of Biblical interpretation which
made the Book more divine by making it
more human, lifting the truth of God into
celestial light by showing how its ramifications reached through all the darknesses
and shadows of human life. There, in
a quiet little retreat, among souls kindred
with his own, sits John Frederick Denison
Maurice, seeing deeply, speaking simply,
so throwing himself into his message that
men from the professions, and especially
from the legal profession, gathering around
him, got so much of the man that they
could not hold him, but gave him forth
throughout England, and made him one
of the foremost of our theological teachers.
Arthur Penrhyn Stanley, in the Abbey
of Westminster, shedding that sweetness

and light of which Matthew Arnold spoke so much and exhibited so little; George Macdonald, writing novels, but into them throwing the new religious spirit, and interpreting through literature some of the profoundest, some of the loftiest, theological truths; A. J. Scott in Manchester, and Baldwin Brown in London, bringing back to men the great truth about the Fatherhood of God, and making that Fatherhood, instead of the ancient sovereignty, the center of theological systems—these, and the like of these, have all been busy in England during the Victorian era, teaching, enlarging, sweetening the Church of Christ.

And yet, among them all, not hindmost, but foremost, was the man who was pastor of this church; foremost in thought-leadership and influence, because speaking to men as preacher, not as mere academic student, not as mere recluse reading books and thinking thoughts in silence, but as a preacher who had seen visions, and dreamed dreams, and gripped problems, and found

out new ways to emancipation and progress.
Beecher thus shines as one of the brightest
stars of our modern firmament, one of the
beautifulest of the gifts of God to these
later days,

What shall we say was his precise contribution to this manifold and greatly enriched age ? I will say, in the first place,
Beecher's greatest work was that he helped
to bring back Christendom to the realization
and enjoyment of the living Christ. Do
not misapprehend my meaning, or imagine
that I am implying an absence of Christ
from the generations that went before ours.
Not even theologies could banish Christ out
of the world into which he had once come
as Redeemer; and he has been here through
all the ages, living and working with men.
But, alas! how often has Christ been here,
as God was with Cyrus of old, girding him,
yet unknown by him, undiscerned by him.
It sometimes seems to me that the mediæval
epochs of Christian life are well represented
in that Disciples' walk to Emmaus with the

Master, when, with glowing heart, they knew they were in the presence of a great teacher, but with holden eyes they did not see him, did not know him.

Beecher's work has been to open men's eyes to the fact that He who makes the star to glow, He who lifts the hopes and purposes of Christendom, is none other than the Son of God, and that he is not dead but risen and living; and that He who lives and sits upon the throne descends and dwells with us, nearer to us than breathing, closer than hands or feet.

Very early in the story of the Christian church did Christ come to be more of a historic person than of a Living Presence, more of a dim and distant reminiscence on the page of history than a deliverer and companion standing by our side. The Roman Catholic Church, to which with reverence and with thankfulness I personally acknowledge deep debts of gratitude for many things bright and beautiful, yet did this wrong to Christendom, that it placed

itself between the believer and his Lord,
and taught men to look for Christ in a
sensuous sacrament, in a visible priest, in
a ritual service, and created, however un-
wittingly, in the thought of Christendom,
this feeling, that only *there* could Christ be
found; that outside of those sacred walls
men walked and worked, and fought and
suffered, without his close companionship
and inspiration.   And when, in due course,
Luther arose in his might, with a waiting
and willing Europe at his back, to smite the
shackles of the Catholic Church from the
neck of Christendom, alas, alas! men went
and put the Bible where the Pope had put
the Church—put there the Bible, and doctrines springing from the Bible—and re-
created a sense of limitation in the spiritual
universe, causing men to think and believe
that in the Book and nowhere else could
they find Christ or learn anything about
him, and that in the doctrines of the Church
they had the embodiment, such as it was,
of the Master's presence with his people.

And so the Church struggled on, weakened and limited by these false conceptions of Christ, and of the way to Christ, until in our own age, from every quarter of the compass, hungering souls cried out for the Living God, for the Christ who said that he would come back again and dwell in his church and with his people; and foremost among those called to interpret this cry of the heart and to guide men to the Living Saviour was Henry Ward Beecher, who himself had found the way, and whose whole life and preaching exhibited the reality, the closeness, the sacredness of communion with Christ.

In one of those matchless epigrammatic passages that brighten so many of the pages of James Martineau, I found one day this little gem of definition: "Complete unbelief is attained when God is driven as much out of the past as we have driven him out of the present; and complete belief is reached when God is made to fill the present as much as piety causes him to fill the past.'' No truer word has been spoken to this generation than that. To fill this present with the living God; to have the courage and the truth to say that if God is not here in Brooklyn he never was in Jerusalem; that if he did not speak by his gifted prophet here, he had nothing to say to Abraham, nothing to David, nothing to Isaiah, and nothing to Paul; and that if he be not here a living inspiration, to comfort and to quicken and to bless, the whole story of his unveiling in the past is one vast but beautiful fiction, to be buried henceforth from the thoughts of men — that is the truth and the duty of this present time. And Beecher led us in England, as he led you in America, to see God and to know that Christ is present, to see the lineaments of his face, to bask in the light of his spirit, and to feel all care and worry and weakness and limitation removed by the saving and emancipating touch of Christ in the heart.

Out of this great truth, which Beecher

taught us to recover, came another truth—namely, that the sources of theology are not to be found in books, not even in sacred books, but in Christian experience. Having found the Living Christ and recognized him, having come into personal communion with him and felt the glow of the heart, and the broadening of the vision, and the sweetening of the temper, and the quickening of all the perceptive and appreciative faculties, it was an easy and a necessary step to the conclusion that here are the great facts on which theology is built, out of which theology must be formed. As the scientist goes to nature for his facts, and proceeds by methods of induction from observed facts to necessary conclusions, so, said Beecher, the theologian must come into the realm of Christian facts, discoverable in the great body of Christian experience, and must by the same inductive methods argue from these facts to what is true about God and what is true about man and duty.

It is true that the scientific student must

have his class-book, must study his class-book, and by it be guided where to look for his facts and how to treat them when he finds them. And so we have *our* text-book, this Bible of God, this book of man, and in addition to it we have our volumes of church history, and we have our histories of Christian doctrine and Christian method. Yet these are but guides, pointing us to where we shall find the great verifying facts, and teaching us how to deal with them, and what to make of them when we find them. Do you tell me that such a basis for theology is uncertain ? that the experience of one man may differ widely from the experience of another man ?   That is true; for if out of mere individual experiences we were to attempt the construction of a theology, we should reach conclusions as confused and as misleading as would be those of the scientist if he attempted, out of a little fact here and a little fact yonder, to construct a great scientific theory.   Our induction must be from all the facts.   My experience must be attested by yours, yours and mine by that of a great company, that of a great company to-day by that of a great company which went before us. When so attested and so confirmed, it will be found that the great realities of religion are written in the hearts and souls of men; and that through a broad induction from them we must arrive at our beliefs in theology. Mr. Beecher's theology was not made up out of books, did not constitute itself in propositions; it was the living interpretation of facts which he observed and of experiences which he shared.

And so it comes to pass, if you will allow me one illustration, that Henry Ward Beecher put before the church a doctrine of the Deity of Jesus Christ, which to me seems absolutely irrefutable. He did not merely gather texts strewn here and there over the Biblical page, and piece them together, and say, " This book tells me that he was God, and I must believe it because the Book says it." No, he went back into his own experience, into the experience of the Christian Church. And what did he find ? He found there unmistakably a great yearning after God, a yearning so deep and persistent that only one thing could be concluded—that God put it there, and put it there as a ground of expectation that he would answer the craving he had created. And out of that came clearly and necessarily the conclusion that the God who made man thus to need and to yearn after himself must answer him, must come to him, or cease to be God—become indeed Diabolus, not to be worshiped, however strong, but to be rejected and repelled as one who made the soul only to mock it and to destroy it by delusion and despair. Thus it was that, arguing from Christian experience, Beecher learned that it was reasonable and obligatory for the God who made man to come to him, and speak to him, and work for him, and die for him. Then, bringing these observations and reasonings to the light of the Scriptural revelation, and looking at the historic Christ from the standpoint of human cravings and needs, Beecher could not escape the conclusion that the Christ portrayed in the Gospels was God's answer to man's necessity. And in grateful surprise he cried: " Why, this is God. There is not a single thing I would have in God but I find in Christ. There is not a single thing in Christ I would not like to have in God. This is, this must be, God. I worship and I adore."

That is an illustration of the new method in theology, largely inaugurated by Henry Ward Beecher. Do you not see how much more powerful, how much more conclusive, it is ? Take any number of texts and prophecies and Messianic hopes written here in the Book, and you cannot build up a theory from them which you will not sometimes doubt and sometimes reject. But build up your theories from Christian experience, and you have an absolutely invulnerable castle of truth in which to live and breathe and work. This, then, was Beecher's second contribution to modern Christian thought—to teach us where to find the sources of our theology.

I cannot do more than merely indicate the effects which flowed from these two great contentions and contributions. Will you note, then, in passing, that this method of Beecher's made theology an intensely vital and interesting study—the most vital and interesting of all studies ?

When I was a youth at college, the most popular thing to say in class was that the study of theology had decayed, and that only intellectual fossils engaged themselves in its pursuit. It would be a shame unspeakable for any man in England to say that to-day. For theology has become the very center of all studies; and men are turning to it from every walk in life, as to that which most satisfies, most repays, most instructs. And the secret of it is that the theology which used to be studied was studied from books; the theology that has now won and held the intellect of Christendom is a theology studied from life.

In the second place, this method supplied the elements of certainty in religion. It threw men back upon the witness which God has placed within themselves, and lifted them, as to the certainty of their faith, above the reach of any criticism or any new development of thought. In England, except in few and inconsiderable places, it would be impossible to-day to raise any alarm, to create any heresy-hunt, because a man brought before Christendom some results of Biblical criticism, or some new interpretation of any of the great doctrines of the faith. Why? Because men have come to see that whether Jonah is a fact or a fiction does not matter; that the spiritual and ethical truth in the story is the thing of importance; that whether Moses wrote the Pentateuch or not is of infinite unimportance, except as a matter of literary interest, so long as the great unfolding of the Divine Will is seen to be unmistakable

and divine; and because men have come to
see that the credibility of Christian truth
finds warrant in the heart and souls of men,
and not in the mere maintenance of historic
propositions and theological theories. And
so it has come to pass that we in England—
I do not know how it is in America—that
we in England live very calmly amid the
busy development of scientific theory, amid
the busier activities of Biblical criticism,
amid the rearrangement of doctrinal truth.
We are very calm, because we know that
He in whom we live and trust is in us and
with us. We know him. We do not
know merely about him: we know him.
We walk with him. We let him come
into the heart. There is glow, there is
sunshine, there is brightness, there is hope,
where he is. And so we say, " Do what
you will with the mechanics of religion, you
cannot take him away from us; he is
crucified in us afresh every day; he rises
afresh in us every day; and, when we are
willing, he sends Pentecosts of glow and

power into our expectant souls. We *know* him because we *have* him; and our faith is sure.''

The time has passed, and I must now content myself with saying in conclusion that I have laid no particular stress in this review upon Beecher's specific contributions to this or that form of Christian doctrine. I have done more, or attempted to do more: I have tried to show that he has influenced the whole spirit of theology and the whole attitude of Christian thought. Calvin's name is identified with the doctrine of Sovereignty, Luther's with the doctrine of Justification, Wesley's with the doctrine of Sanctification. You will never be able to identify the name of Beecher with any one single doctrine. But this we do in England —this I trust and believe you do in America: we feel that this man held so much of God in him, and recognized so clearly the grace that had saved him, as to bring into the whole realm of theologic thought a new spirit, a new outlook, which

broke down ancient superstitions, and made
the way clear for men to work in new con-
structions, solid and beautiful, of Christian
truth and Christian hope. His was the
influence of leaven in the meal. Sometimes
it is the fate—shall I not say it is the glory?
—of such workers as he, soon to be lost on
the page of history as a mere name, and to
live, as he often longed to live in life,
obscure, unnoticed of men, with his work
for his joy and his Master for his reward.
But whether the name of Beecher goes
down on the page of history as one of the
creative personalities or not, of this I am
assured: his spirit will go down, and it will
be a spirit making for peace, breadth,
charity, yea, a spirit making for the recognition of Christ, the love of Christ, the surrender of the heart to Christ, and issuing
through that surrender into emancipation
and enlargement of thought, of service, of
personal and sacred experience.

Accept, then, my friends, these fragmen-
tary utterances of one who knew and loved

your pastor, and who knew and loved him
well enough to know that, as he is here with
us to-day, he is well content at the absence
of mere personal eulogy, and at the exaltation of those great truths and wise methods
for which he pleaded. Mr. Beecher is gone
from you, and gone from the world, as a
corporeal presence; but his influence still
lives and operates in many hearts and lands.
Here in this building, where the echoes of
his voice still linger, that influence is
obvious and potent. Beyond this building,
outreaching even the expansive coasts of
this vast continent, that influence is not less
effective because less specifically recogniz-
able. He lives, here where he was known,
beyond, where he was not known, in the
work he accomplished, in the thoughts he
uttered, in the spirit he breathed. But if
he is to continue to live, it must be through
you, and through us who caught so many
inspirations from his heart. And the most
permanent, as it will be the most honoring,
memorial we can rear to him will be to obey

as well as learn his teaching, and to trans-
late into renewed and sanctified life the
credible and beautiful Gospel which he
preached with such power and exhibited
with such grace during forty sacred years in
this house.

The Theological Problem for To-Day.

GEORGE A. GORDON.

IV.

The Theological Problem for To=Day.[1]

By the Rev. GEORGE A. GORDON, D.D.,
Of Old South Congregational Church, Boston, Mass.

THE strange thing that confronts one almost everywhere to-day is the absence of theology in the supreme sense of that word. For all thinking men who are in any measure open to the new light and spirit of our time, Calvinism as an adequate interpretation of the ways of God with men, or even as a working philosophy in life, is forever gone. And thus far nothing equally elaborate and commanding has arisen to take its place. There has been a great negation of one theology, without, in the deepest sense,

---

[1] Plymouth Church, Brooklyn, Thursday, November 11, 1897.

143

an equally great affirmation of another. We can imagine a parallel. We can imagine an explosion and rejection of the Ptolemaic system of astronomy without the introduction into the vacant place of the Copernican. That the sun and planets do not revolve round the earth we can suppose that men have become absolutely certain; that this little globe of ours is not the center of the universe is clear; that what are called sunrise and sunset are but appearances can no longer be doubted. But nothing further is settled. No map of the heavens to replace the old one has yet been made. No scheme of the real center and movements of the planetary system has yet been elaborated. Nothing exists but single thoughts, isolated discoveries, promising insights that so far have not been wrought over into one comprehensive and sovereign conception. The old astronomy, with its appeal to sense and its wonderful hold upon the popular imagination, is gone, and the new, in anything like scientific shape, has not arrived.

If we can imagine the men of the fifteenth century as having lost Ptolemy without having found Copernicus, we shall have a parallel for the condition of things in theology to-day. In proof of this statement, I ask you to recall the chief fields of theological interest at the present time. History, criticism, interpretation—of these we have an unprecedented supply. The annals of the race, literary and institutional, secular and religious, have been read with an eagerness, an intelligence, and with the application of scientific methods absolutely unparalleled. The text, the composition, the times and environments of the Old Testament and the New have been the subject of amazing and fruitful activity. The same is true of the entire history of the Christian church. And antiquity as the source of beginnings has wielded a wonderful fascination over thousands of scholars. Upon history, criticism, interpretation, the representative library of to-day is full of new books, and one can have nothing but praise for the splendid achievement embodied in them. The limitation, however, is strikingly obvious. One looks almost in vain for books giving an elaboration into coherent and commanding form of the new ideas by which Christian men are living. The new ideas lie in our life with the most confusing and provoking miscellaneousness. We cry out for order. The house of faith must be rebuilt; and for the last five and twenty years scholars the world over have done nothing but collect materials. David was allowed to make a contribution to the house of the Lord for his time, but he was not permitted to build it, because he had been a man of war and had shed much blood. It may be that a similar prohibition, for a similar reason, has been served upon the critical scholars of our time. They have been men of war; they have shed much blood; and if they should construct an edifice for faith, perhaps the generation still smarting under the wounds it has received might refuse to enter.

Others may think that the parallel to these historical scholars is Saul and not David. It is because of compromise with an evil system, because of foolish unwillingness to shed more blood, that they have lost their throne. At all events, the house of faith remains to be built. We have materials in abundance, old and new, but the building is not in sight. If any man shall say, We need none, because we have a building of God, a house not made with hands, eternal in the heavens, he is simply mistaking the eternal pattern in the Mount for the tabernacle below that it is still incumbent upon the spiritual intelligence to raise for the service and solace of all the journeying children of God. Books on theology proper, works dealing with ideas and organizing them into a great and commanding whole, are lamentably few. It is so much easier to dig than to construct, to be intellectual hod-carriers than to be architects and builders of the habitation of the spirit.

A further confirmation of this contention

may be had from a national instance. Five and twenty years ago Calvinism was dominant from one end of Scotland to the other. To-day it is dominant nowhere; it has, indeed, been utterly outgrown and left behind. What has effected this great change ? Chiefly the new Biblical scholarship, and not philosophical thinking. Professor Davidson, of Edinburgh, that quiet, shrewd, fascinating, resistless old scholar and maker of scholars, is behind it all. His greatest pupil, W. Robertson Smith, made an epoch in the national life of Scotland by his learning, and not by any departure from Calvinism. Others have risen up and carried forward the work that he, with so much ability and courage, inaugurated. Hundreds of young leaders are to-day spreading the light. A corresponding movement has been running, during most of this time, in New Testament interpretation. For years Professor A. B. Bruce, revered as a great teacher of the New Testament, as much in America as in Great Britain, was almost a solitary light. Now he is the center of an ever-growing brotherhood of like-minded men. The thing to be noted is that in the accomplishment of this wonderful revolution in the belief of a nation very little purely theological thinking has appeared. The light has come in through history, criticism, exegesis; the old scheme has been expelled by a new body of knowledge, and a fresh mass of nobler religious feeling. Still, it must be said that in Scotland to-day there is really no philosophical theology, no theory of Christianity, and man's religious life worked out in fundamental opposition to the rejected Calvinism. Scotland waits for a theology to fill the vacant throne.

The same thing meets us at home. How many diligent, learned, and brilliant workmen we have in fields that pass under the general name of theology it would be impossible to say. Nor would it be possible to do them too much honor. All our theological schools, or nearly all, are centers of fresh and fruitful activity; many of our colleges and universities are in touch with the same spirit. But the movement has hardly got beyond the question of literature. It is the work of the scholar rather than the thinker; it is the gathering of knowledge rather than the organization of ideas. No one can value too highly these preliminaries; but preliminaries should have a tendency to become finals, tributaries should at least move onward toward the main stream, the interests of the scholar should merge at length in the greater interest of the thinker. And although untold good must continue to come, in many ways and for many ends, from Biblical scholarship, it is at least questionable if we have not already reached the permanent conception of the nature and office of the Holy Scriptures. They are simply the supreme literature of the religious life, and their authority, as in the teachings of Christ, is the authority of the highest of their kind. Historical criticism is, after all, a matter of environment; the content of the Bible, the word of God there, is the object

of the enlightened human spirit. We need
no longer delay our new building era on
account of the Bible. Its hewn stones rest-
ing upon the chief corner-stone are already
here and in place.

The absence of a theology giving intellectual form and justification to the better
sentiment of the time is abundantly visible
in our ministry. Among almost all our
effective preachers the sympathies are
modern; but in the greater number the
theology is either ancient or non-existent.
In either case, the mass of prevailing emo-
tion and practical activity has no corresponding body of ideas in league with it.
The scheme entertained is usually some
decrepit modification of the Calvinistic kind,
too long idle for effective service, with the
courage but without the capacity for battle;
while the purposes, sentiments, and practical outlooks are all of this new and greater
day. We are full of joy so long as we are
permitted to feel with these brethren; but
the moment we hear them speak their

philosophy, our bewilderment is like that of
the patriarch of old. The hands are the
hands of Esau; so far, so good. But the
voice is the voice of Jacob: here comes in
the endless confusion. How often does one
see the old theology unconsciously dressing
itself up in the garments of the new, with
unreflecting simplicity covering the parts
that would surely betray it, and advancing
guilelessly in borrowed enthusiasms and
simulated loves to obtain dominion over the
blind ! The success is but for the moment;
the old supplanting character cannot long
be concealed.

Now, the chief theological necessity for
to-day I take to be the rebuilding of the
edifice of Christian belief. We need a
temple for the intelligence. We need fundamental and ruling ideas set in the strength
of their own natural order. We need an
intellectual basis for the new faith, passion,
and enterprise of the Church of Christ in
our time. As will be seen, I can indicate
but a single line of thought upon this vast

subject. Christian thinkers are under bonds to find in God the secure foundation for all human interests, the assurance of a divine intention and grace adequate to the need and capacity of mankind. We must first of all command the point where the life of Christianity itself is involved. And this is the point whose importance the entire history of Plymouth Church illustrates, in support of which it has stood these fifty years, and round which has toiled, with prophetic insight, magnificent insistence, and beneficent results to the whole country, the genius both of its first minister and its second.

1. Calvinism is right in its claim that the being of God is the supreme interest both in theology and life. This is the note of greatness, sounding clearer as the generations pass, in the thought of Augustine, Calvin, and Edwards. Jonathan Edwards, because of his devouring passion for God as the absolutely perfect, is bright with an everlasting light. The new movement in

theology, conscious as it is of revolutionary
intent, is here at one with all true theology.
It aims to behold all things in God. Its
hope is to begin, continue, and end in God.
Its source in all its genuine representatives
is the aboriginal necessity of the human
soul: " My heart and my flesh cry out for
the living God."

But Christian thinkers are learning that
there are two great abuses of this sublime
passion. Willingness to be damned for the
glory of God may be the sign of a humble
spirit; but it is in reality the supreme insult
to God. For it assumes that the glory of
God and the weal of man are incompatible
interests. To exalt God so high as to
banish him from the world is a terrible
error. To refuse to see God in the natural
life of men is to take the first step toward
atheism. For a God wholly above the
world-process, wholly apart from the normal
interests of men, wholly transcendent, is
practically no God at all. In Carlyle's
phrase, such a God " does nothing," and

for human beings he is nothing. This is
the inevitable outcome of the belief that
makes God too good to be in the world,
that makes the world too wicked to have
the presence of God in it. The other
abuse is one peculiar to our century. It
lies in identifying God with the development of human history, in refusing to see
that God is at the same time in all and over
all.

Against this twofold error of a God
wholly above the world, and a God completely one with its process, the theology
for to-day must do battle. The acorn falls
into the ground. The plan of the tree is
there. That plan lives in the acorn, and
yet transcends it. It bursts the acorn in
the soil, runs it out into new and wondrous
forms, drives it up through the earth, sends
it higher and higher, and through the discipline of a thousand years it struggles to live
more and more in the tree. And when the
tree has come to its best; when it is deepest
in the earth, highest in the air, and widest

in the sweep of its great arms, the ideal of the tree still looks beyond. The wondrous product still falls short of perfection, and therefore the plan is still a beautiful excess even upon the tree at its best. This is the Christian idea of God. He is in the organism of humanity from the first. It is he that sends the race into all its growths. It is he that gives man ideals, and that fills his heart with achieving power. It is he that brings men into families that grow sweeter with the centuries; that sets these families in nations that slowly ascend in character; that moves the nations into wider federations of trade and art and science; that lights up the future with the dream of universal brotherhood; that compels the race to leave more and more of its brutehood behind it; and that, with a sublime insistence, urges it on upon the full realization of its humanity. We have an indwelling God, a God whose indwelling is the fountain of our whole character and hope. But we have a God above and beyond the process of human society, a God whose character is an eternal excess upon human history, a God who can never live wholly in man because he is so infinitely great in wisdom and love for man. God lives eternally in his own plan, in his own ideal, in his own love. He lives for himself because he represents in himself the inconceivable good in reserve for mankind. Thus we must strive to combine in our thought of God the primary truth in Calvinism—the infinite exaltation of God, and the fundamental insight of our century—God's presence in all human history.

2. I have said that Calvinism is profoundly right in concentrating human interest upon God. It is right in its fundamental contention concerning God. The final thing in the universe is the Divine Will. Calvinism is wrong, grievously wrong in the character that it ascribes to that ultimate Will. If that Will be against the greater part of mankind, as Calvinism declares, nothing can long keep us from

despair; but if that Will be for us, as a true theology must contend, who can be against us? The fundamental position of the traditional theology does not admit a God for mankind. The new superstructure of sentiment cannot stand upon the old theological basis. The scheme of salvation which has, with a few noble exceptions, prevailed in the Church from the days of Augustine to the present time, the theory against which Henry Ward Beecher revolted, and which he fought with the power of a world-shaker, never dreamed of God as seriously caring for all mankind. There was antiquity, but only the Hebrew people were of concern to God. A few great souls might possibly be recovered from the general wreck, like Cyrus and Socrates, Plato and Plutarch, Epictetus and Marcus Aurelius; but, as a whole, antiquity did not lie in the gracious purpose of God. It had died to him in Adam, and he had not even cared to try to make it live to him in Christ. There were the nations contemporaneous with the

Christian Church in its development. They were material from which a selection was made; but as nations, as communities of human beings, they were not included in God's moral regard for the world. There were the heathen peoples, the belated rear-guard of mankind, the millions who had been obstructed in the onward march, detained in the swamps fighting the beast in its earlier and uglier forms. In the dust and heat of this modern day they began to roll in sight. What was to be thought concerning them? Again the same scheme was applied. Their entire past was regarded as Godless; the myriads of their predecessors, those whom these races looked upon as heroic and pious ancestors, had gone irrevocably to their doom. These peoples themselves are but fresh material for the selective purpose of the Highest; and through the message of the missionary he will choose whom he will, and reject whom he will. The old theology had two superlative merits; it was honest, and it was courageous. It did not try to appear other than the terrible partialism that it was. It did not shrink from the avowal of its own logic.

That is the scheme which has fallen from the control of the Church, and to whose vacant throne no contrasted conception of equal thoroughness and vigor has yet come. And it is precisely this ultimate origin of the new theology to which I would turn attention. The new scheme is not founded upon sentiment; it is not the product of benevolent dreamers; it is not held blindly in spite of human nature, the movement of history, the spirit of the New Testament, the order of the moral world, the heart of the universe. The old scheme was great in its confidence that the facts were on its side and against the nobler view. Nothing could be further from the truth. The older theology saw the sternness of life, but it did not understand Paul's exclamation, "Behold the goodness and the severity of God!" Its hopeless outlook upon the world was due to limitation of vision. As Phillips Brooks has taught us in one of his noblest sermons, it is easy to curse life if only a part is seen. Balak was shrewd enough to see that if Balaam was to find himself able to curse Israel, he must look upon the part, the utmost part, the wretchedest part, and not upon the magnificent whole.

3. The theology for to-day must found itself upon the will of God, and upon the will of God at its highest. When we look for God in the cosmic order, we can do little until we find man there. Man, as the crown of the cosmic process, shows that process at its best, shows what lies behind it all. When we look for God in man, we do little until we find Christ, the Ideal Man. In Christ man the creature is at his best, and God the Creator is at his best. The incarnation is the center of all sane theology. Man at his best can alone give us God at his best. To this issue the supreme divinity of Christ comes. Jesus took the Infinite at his best; that is, he took God as he was in

his Son.   Unless we look at his model, the
genius of the architect can be known only
from his building; and his character will
share in the confusion of the process.   Unless we look at Christ, the typal man, we
can judge the Maker of our human world
only by what we see.   And only when God
shall have made the pile complete can our
judgment be final.   Therefore we build
upon Christ as the sublime anticipation of
perfected humanity, as the archetypal man
standing complete in the confusion of the
great historic construction, and giving us
through man at his best God at his best.
We must therefore revise all other revela-
tions of God in nature, in the constitution
of man, in human history, and in the Holy
Scriptures themselves, by the light that falls
from the glory of God in the face of Jesus
Christ.   Nothing must be allowed to con-
tradict the essential meaning of the Incarnation.   It stands for the eternal goodness of
God in the inexpressible sternness of the
process of history.   If the Incarnation is

not to be lost from faith, if the mission of Christ is not to be reduced to a delusion, if Christianity is not to be contracted into the religion of a sect, the saving purpose of God in Christ must be made to cover the race.

It is true that this principle is revolutionary. The affirmation that God has a Christian purpose toward our entire humanity involves an extension of the field of redemption so enormous as to make obsolete, at a single stroke, the whole theological map of the traditional view. And what seems worse, while all clear-seeing men are aware that this does not necessarily imply universal salvation, it is true that it looks that way. *If God shall succeed*, universal salvation will be the final result. And this sounds so perilous to good morals, and seems to cut the nerve of all strenuous endeavor! O my brothers, when will Christian thinkers fear atheism more than universalism, when will they see that the deepest immorality lies in distrust of the righteous will of God, when will they awake to the fact that only those who believe in a God for humanity and eternally for humanity can resist unto blood! Any scheme that puts God with an inclusive and everlasting purpose of redemption behind mankind, looks like universalism; but let us remember that any other scheme is, in our time, a royal road to atheism. When we assert, as we do so easily, the brotherhood of man, let us be sure that the universe, according to our view, is not against it; let us be sure that there is in God a universal fatherhood upon which to found it.

4. One more specification must be made. Where in the new scheme of theological thought does the Christian doctrine of the Holy Spirit come in? About no other truth of the Christian faith is there, among good people, so much serious and profound conviction and so much vagueness. Still every Christian heart knows when its treasure is rightly named. It knows when the point is met and when it is missed. It will not accept a stone for bread, nor a scorpion for

an egg. The philosophical idea of the immanence of God is not the Christian doctrine of the Holy Spirit. The life of God in the souls of the Hebrew prophets and in the hearts of the outside saints, as Dr. Bushnell calls them, the divine indwelling represented by the ethnic religions át their best, or by the Hebrew faith at its highest, is not what the disciple of Christ means when he speaks of the Holy Spirit. There is indeed a profound identity in the two experiences, but there is a difference equally profound. God is the same God, and yet the Christian revelation brings to light the hidden character of God. The Christian conception of God as the God and Father of our Lord Jesus Christ is so ineffably great that God looks through it upon the believer, and comes through it in upon the heart of the individual and the Church in ways and measures and powers altogether new.

The doctrine of the Holy Spirit is the coming of the life of the God and Father of Jesus Christ. God as he comes through the historic Christ, as he finds the form of his coming in Christ, as he is seen and felt and experienced through Christ, is the Holy Spirit of our faith. The Christian idea of the Holy Spirit is inseparable from the Christian thought of Christ. A supreme historic character reveals the ineffable love of God, and continues the everlasting form of God for the Christian mind, the channel along which God evermore comes to the Christian heart, the atmosphere through which God in his light and grace comes and lives in the Christian life.

It is indeed the Christian God who made the heavens and the earth, who made our world the abode of life, who filled life with ceaseless aspiration and endowed it with the force that through ascending forms seeks its consummation in man. It is the Christian God who made all men of one blood, who left no people altogether without witness of himself, who through lower religions and higher has spoken to the human soul, who has given man a moral nature, an ideal of fellowship in the family and in the total interests of existence, who has constituted our humanity in his own image, smitten it with an immortal hunger for himself, and moved upon it from the beginning in the tides of his love. It is the Christian God who has made our human world and the universe in which it is set; but men did not know it and could not know it until Christ came. The immanent God is known in Christ as our Father; but not until he is thus known can we date the coming of the Holy Spirit. The Pentecostal vision of God, and life and power under God, were mediated by the Lord Jesus Christ. Because he is the final and perfect mediator of God, we know God as the Holy Spirit. Therefore is the Holy Spirit the Christian Indweller, the Christian Comforter. He is the light of the Christian intelligence, the strength of the Christian will, the rapture of the Christian heart, the Ineffable in the Christian life. He is the reserve of God bestowed alone upon those who look to him through our Master, Christ.

Here, then, is the issue of all that I have said to-night. I have insisted upon a metaphysical insight, an ethical faith, a historical fact, and a supreme experience. I have contended for the insight that finds a God in all and over all; for the faith that holds to the absolute goodness of the Infinite Will; for the historical fact that becomes the supreme interpretation both of the Divine intention and human capacity; and for the exalted experience in which all truth finds its field and power. Immanence and transcendence must meet in the nature of the Ineffable God, the righteousness of God must come to sovereign expression in the Incarnation of the Son of God, and the prophetic character of the Incarnation must advance toward fulfillment in the Christian life. The metaphysical insight must issue in the ethical faith, both insight and faith must find verification in the history of Jesus Christ, and upon this must begin the dis-

pensation of the Holy Spirit, the perpetual
coming of the Christian God in the life of
mankind.

For the individual the message from the
theology here indicated is that salvation is
righteousness. Whatever truth there may
be in the ideas of imputation, substitution,
vicarious sacrifice—and I am glad to be able
to see a world of noble meaning in them—
they do not in any way conflict with the
fact that righteous character, and nothing
else, is salvation; that character is the
achievement of the personal will; that it can
be won, in the deepest sense, only by the
soul for itself; that God himself cannot
bestow it except through the agony and
bloody sweat of the human spirit. The
path of eternal life is the path of anguish;
tears are its meat day and night while it
hears the world cry, "Where is thy God?"
The stress of heart in the soul that is gain-
ing new standing in the truth, winning new
interests in the kingdom of God, and making new advances upon righteousness cannot

be put into words. There are none but heroic feet upon that stairway of fire. Idlers and pretenders, soft and luxurious lives, have no place in that awful but blessed process. Salvation for the moral shirk, while he remains a shirk, God in his mercy has made forever impossible.

But this is not the final word. To the question shot upward from the hearts of the brave in the strenuousness and seeming impossibility of the righteous life, Is God for us or against us? there must be but one answer. We must not make God responsible for the continuance of iniquity. We must define sin as resistance to the realization of the righteous purpose of God in the soul. God is against the race only when it is against itself; and in that case his wrath is his mercy. God is on the side of every man who sets his heart on righteousness. The deepest in human nature, in human society, in human history, in the course of the world, in the on-going universe, makes for the seeker after righteousness. The

stars in their courses fight for the man who
contends for a pure heart; and to every soul
face to face with the tremendousness of the
moral process the sublime comfort comes,
"The Eternal God is thy refuge, and underneath are the everlasting arms."

The Social Problems of the Future.

WASHINGTON GLADDEN.

V.

The Social Problems of the Future.

By the Rev. WASHINGTON GLADDEN, D.D.,[1]
Of First Congregational Church, Columbus, O.

I BRING to you to-night, my friends of
Plymouth Church, no better offering than
that which can be expressed in the pulsa-
tions of a heart that beats in unison with
yours as you recall the toils and the gains,
the battles and the victories, of the last fifty
years. In all the larger life of this memorable era this church has borne a worthy
part. The prudent man hesitates to compare the efficiency of moral causes, or to
employ superlatives in estimating the forces
that work for righteousness; but I shall risk

---

[1] Plymouth Church, Brooklyn, Thursday, November 11, 1897.

nothing in saying that we are standing in a place from which light and power have radiated to the ends of the earth. In shaping the thought of this Nation and in leavening its life, Plymouth Church has been and is one of the potent influences. It is impossible for you to recall and re-count, as you have been doing for the last few days, the history of the last fifty years, without deep and solemn thankfulness to God for the tasks which he has put upon this church, and the work that he has wrought by means of it.

If Plymouth Church has stood for one thing more clearly than for anything else, it has been the idea that Christianity gives the law to the whole of life; that it must control our business, our politics, our pleasures; that Jesus Christ is Lord of capital and counting-room, of factory and studio, of school and home. It was this resolute purpose to apply the Christian law to all our social relations that made the Plymouth pulpit the power that it was in the great conflict which issued in the war and the emancipation of the slaves. How strange and far away seems the day when this testimony began to be uttered in Plymouth Church—not here alone, but here more clearly and convincingly than almost anywhere else. It was not the popular thing to say in those days; men who were looking for promotion found something else to talk about. To insist that the slave was our brother, and that we had no right to make merchandise of him, was an offense against all decencies and proprieties. Well do I remember a prayer in the church which was nurse of my childish faith, a prayer wherein the young minister made bold to pray "for our brethren in bonds as bound with them;" and how the faces of the elders reddened with indignation because politics had been brought into their pulpit! That minister went; he was not allowed to stand upon the order of his going. And the same temper quite generally prevailed. To insist upon the clear declaration of the doctrine that God is the Father of all men was to expose yourself to accusations of sensationalism and sedition and even of heresy. It was clearly proved, from some influential pulpits, that abolitionism and infidelity were one and the same thing. That was the kind of Christianity that Plymouth pulpit had to meet and fight; and there was no faltering. These walls began to echo with words of power that stirred the conscience and the manhood of the whole Nation. If they could only give back to us to-night a few of the trumpet-calls with which they have resounded!

I remember well—it is not possible that I should ever forget—what seemed to me the culmination of this mighty testimony, in the Thanksgiving sermon preached here thirty-seven years ago this month — in November, 1860, immediately after the election of Abraham Lincoln. The Legislature of South Carolina had already called a convention to dissolve the Union, and the air was full of the mutterings of secession.

The house was crowded. And what a reaffirmation we heard that day of the great truth of human brotherhood, of which these political movements were the passionate repudiation! I sat up there, in that left-hand gallery, against the wall, and listened to what I have always felt was the most tremendous speech I ever heard. How the house rocked and swayed with the glorious passion! There were thunderings and lightning and voices; there were hailstones and coals of fire. "I would die myself," cried the prophet, "cheerfully and easily, before a man should be taken out of my hands when I had the power to give him liberty and the hound was after him for his blood. I would stand as an altar of expiation between slavery and liberty, knowing that, through my example, a million men would live. A heroic deed, in which one yields up his life for others, is his Calvary. It was the hanging of Christ on the hill-top that made it the highest mountain on the globe."

And then again: "I stand to declare that justice is worth more than all the corn-fields of the continent. I stand to declare that right between man and man is worth more than all the freights of all the ships that whiten the sea. I stand to declare that there is not in the king's crown, nor in the scepter of any monarch, such a power as there is in simple mercy between human beings. I stand to declare that the secret of national compactness is in national conscience, national affection, and national faith in moral ideas. And I stand to declare that the period in which men scoff at moral laws and moral truths is a period of rank infidelity and utter apostasy. The form of religion may stand in such a period, but it will be worm-eaten; it will be dead; it will be rotten. And if you want to know which way nations are to go to find prosperity, let me tell you that every nation that means to be prospered must steer straight to the lighthouse of God's universe. And what is that? God's heart. Any nation that steers for any other thing will run upon rocks and shoals.''

Such were the great deliverances of that memorable day. Such has always been the testimony of Plymouth Church; thank God that it is as clear and strong to-day as ever it was! When, therefore, Plymouth Church summons me to speak of the social questions of the future, it is not requiring of me a kind of speech that is novel to this platform. The religion of this church has always been vitally related to the social life of the people. Nor is it needful that I should go in search of any new message. The one great truth of the brotherhood of man is the substance of all I have to say. Nobody can say it more strongly than your pastor has said it: ''All our national problems are problems of human brotherhood.''

You have asked me to speak of social questions; there is but one social question, and that is the question whether,

> '' Man to man, the world o'er,
> Shall brithers be, and a' that.''

Just as soon as men are ready to answer that question heartily, in the affirmative sense, our social problems will disappear as easily as the August sun absorbs the morning mist. To recognize this relation of brotherhood as existing between all human beings, and to accept the truth that every human institution, every law, every form of social organization, must conform to this fundamental fact, is to find the true and complete solution of all the questions that disturb our peace.

Take, for example, the question of taxation. In some of its forms this question has been worn threadbare by discussion; in other of its aspects not nearly so much has been said about it as needs to be said. Beyond doubt a large share of the evils under which we are suffering to-day arise from inequitable taxation. The great majority of good citizens have come to look upon the tax-gatherer as a disturber of their complacency, and upon the levies which he makes as something in the nature of extortion. And, as things now are, there is some justification for this feeling on the part of honest men; for there can be no doubt that, even when direct taxes are considered, the honest man bears far more than his fair share of the burdens of society. What it costs to be honest is brought home to every man who goes to the treasurer's office for his tax-bill. My own opinion is that we have some systems of taxation which are calculated—not perhaps intended —to put the heaviest burdens on those least able to bear them. And it is certain that even under the system of direct taxation the strong and shrewd do contrive to evade a large part of their proper contribution, and that the conscientious are compelled to suffer for the sins of the unscrupulous. This state of things is becoming intolerable and even ominous; dangers to the peace of society are arising in this quarter whose seriousness is not likely to be overstated.

What, now, is the cause of all this? It is

nothing else but the refusal to accept the simple fact of human brotherhood, and to live in true brotherly relations. These schemes by which some classes are burdened for the aggrandizement of others are in contempt of the law of brotherhood. These strong and shrewd citizens who contrive to pay less than their share of the cost of government, knowing well that others must therefore pay more than their share, are not acting the part of brothers. This infraction of the law of Christ, which is the fundamental law of all sound democratic society, is just as real as is that of the slaveholder. The fact that it is less obvious and flagrant, that it is more easily concealed, does not diminish its danger to character or to the social order. It is out of these hidden injustices that the worst mischiefs of society arise.

I have said that a great many good citizens always make this enforced contribution to the common welfare somewhat unwillingly. But if all men were brothers indeed, and, instead of seeking to shirk their burdens and put them on the shoulders of others, were trying to bear one another's burdens, this would be the one expenditure which we should make most cheerfully. For, to say nothing of our consciousness that we were thus ministering to the common good, we should also have the assurance that larger returns would come to ourselves from this outgo than from any other possible investment. If the money paid into the public treasury were honestly and intelligently used for the public welfare, we should receive greater benefit from it than from the same amount employed in any private enterprise. "No money we pay," says Professor Ely, "begins to yield such results as money paid in taxation, provided always that it is prudently expended by a good government. Let a small houseowner in a city like Baltimore, who pays, say, fifty dollars a year in taxes, reflect on what he receives in return. He receives, dollar for dollar, five times as much as for any other expenditure. Streets, libraries, free schools, protection to property and person, including health department, pleasure-grounds royal in their magnificence,—all these are placed at his service. What private corporation ever gave one-fifth as much for the same money?'' All this is possible because of the great economies of co-operation when a whole city joins in the enterprise. And if the principles of taxation were equitably adjusted, so that each one should be called on to bear his fair share of the public burdens according to his ability, and if the citizens, in the spirit of the royal law, heartily responded to this arrangement, each man determining to put upon his brother no part of his own load, taxation would cease to be a problem, and would present to us a welcome opportunity not only of serving our fellows, but of increasing our own happiness.

It may be supposed that this suggestion borders on Utopianism; and, indeed, I have no expectation that it will be entirely adopted in the Greater New York during the coming administration; but I am as fully convinced as I can be of anything that you will never get this problem of taxation solved, with any degree of satisfaction, until you have brought this obligation of brotherhood very distinctly to bear upon it; until you make it perfectly clear, to Christian men at least, that it is just as unbrotherly and un-Christian to make your neighbor pay your taxes as it is to steal his pocketbook or compel him to serve you as a slave. We must, of course, do what we can to frame systems of taxation by which these obligations shall be equitably distributed and impartially enforced; but we shall never get justice done and peace established until the law of brotherhood, instead of the law of conflict, is recognized as the supreme law of the social order.

Monopoly is another of the troublesome facts of the social order. What is monopoly? It is the successful attempt to get the sources of some commodity or service so completely under control that the monopolist can fix his own price upon it. Monopolies of certain kinds of traffic were formerly granted by kings to favored subjects; in later times they are secured by getting possession of lands or mines or patented machinery, or by making such combinations of capital and resources that competition shall be practically impossible. I will not discuss the methods by which monopoly is secured; it is the aim and purpose of it that I am dealing with. And I suppose that the simple purpose is to acquire power which may be used by the monopolist in levying tribute upon the possessions and earnings of his fellow men—in making them enrich him by their labor. The monopolist makes no bargains with those who deal with him; the price is fixed by himself. Economically they are not his equals, they are his dependents. "Give a man power over my subsistence," said Alexander Hamilton, "and he has power over the whole of my moral being." And there are those who do

control, in a large measure, the means of
our subsistence, and who thus possess a
power over our lives which one human being
ought not to assume over the life of another.
Such a power does not consort with brotherhood. It is not in the heart of the brother
to make of his brethren dependents on his
will and servants of his greed or his ambi-
tion. The thought that his wealth is a
tribute that he has had power to enforce
upon those to whom he owes a brother's
love and service would be intolerable to
him. It is true that in many cases the
tribute paid by each is so small that the
oppression is not felt. A profit of one cent
a month out of each of the inhabitants of
this country would not seem large, but it
would give me an income of $8,400,000 a
year. The fact that the exactions of
monopoly are so light has blinded us to its
dangers. For the spirit that can make spoil
of humanity, however cautiously it may
operate, is a spirit which cannot be safely
harbored among men. These tremendous

accumulations of power threaten the very foundations of the social order. "Liberty and monopoly," says Mr. Lloyd, "cannot live together." "When it comes to know the facts, the human heart can no more endure monopoly than American slavery or Roman empire." If brotherhood is the fundamental fact, this must be so, for the law of brotherhood is the precise antithesis of the spirit of monopoly. The one bids me by love serve my neighbor and count his interest my own; the other bids me by craft make my neighbor serve me, while I drain his cistern into my reservoir. It cannot be difficult to see that the essence of the thing which we call monopoly is the very contradiction of the spirit of Christian brotherhood.

Doubtless we must find ways of restraining this power, or controlling it for the good of all. I believe in monopolies; indeed, vast economies are possible by means of them; but I believe that the people should own every one of them and reap these gains, rather than that a few should be enriched at the expense of the many. But the one thing needful is the application to all human relations of the Christian law of brotherhood. It is well if we forbid men thus to lay tribute on one another: but that will avail us little unless we can make them see that such spoliation violates the Christian law as really as does theft or slavery; and that human society cannot rest on secure foundations until the desire to enrich ourselves at the expense of our neighbors is submerged in the nobler wish to make them the sharers in our prosperity and partners in our happiness.

The labor question also is a disquieting business. Between those who organize the world's industries and those who perform them the relations have come to be somewhat strained. On either side there is too much suspicion and ill will; the struggle over the division of the product of labor has developed bad tempers on both sides: at best we have a state of truce in which the combatants tolerate each other; at worst we have conflicts in which each strives to inflict economic injury upon the other, and both, so far as this purpose goes, are uniformly and terribly successful. The amount of harm which the assailants are able to do each other is very great; a considerable part of the poverty and suffering of the land and a much larger part of the unsocial feeling which threaten our peace are due to these labor quarrels. War between civilized men is always in the last degree irrational; these labor wars are no exception to the rule. Every hour of their continuance diminishes the product of industry and reduces the sum of welfare for both employers and employed.

What is the cure for these disorders? Many remedies are suggested, all of which may afford relief. Conciliation, arbitration, profit-sharing, ownership by the workmen of stock in the company which employs them—all these are rational suggestions of methods whose practicability has already, to a considerable extent, been demonstrated. But there is not much use in the temporary conciliation of those who intend to hold themselves in relations which imply hostility; and arbitration connotes enmity. For all these methods, and for every other attempt to find a better way of organizing labor, there is needed first of all the recognition of the fundamental fact of human brotherhood. Those to whom this is a reality have no need to be reconciled; the law of strife has become to them as unnatural as the warfare of the right hand against the left; they are able to see that it is a manifest absurdity for one social class to think to prosper through conflict with other classes.

If men are brethren, and if the most unnatural and monstrous business they can possibly engage in is fighting one another (and that is certainly the doctrine of Jesus Christ), then I see no reason why this truth should not be asserted and insisted on as the only principle that can bear rule in the

realm of labor and capital. I know of
factories where it is really believed and
acted on; I know employers to whom the
truth that the men who work for them are
their brother men, partners of their welfare
and sharers of their prosperity, is just as
palpable as gravitation, and just as thor-
oughly respected. Those are happy factories, you may guess—and prosperous, too,
thank God! They ought to prosper. Is it
really incredible that men should find more
profit in helping one another than in cheat-
ing and fighting one another? To some, to
many, I fear, it is incredible. With the
New Testament in our hands for eighteen
hundred years, we have not yet really
learned to believe that friendship is better
than strife; and we still go on assuming
that the society in which each one is trying
to get all he can away from everybody else,
and to give as little as he can to everybody
else, is the only normal society; that if we
should turn right about and give all we
could to everybody, taking from others only

that which they could freely give, we should speedily find ourselves in the highway to ruin. Is it not curious that reasonable men should not be able to see that by such assumptions the social order is simply inverted as to its leading motive, and that it is high time for those men who have the power to turn the world upside down to come hither also, that they may get it right side up? To all right reason it is so palpable, so utterly common-sensible, that it is cheaper and easier and safer and more profitable for those who are working together to be friends than to be foes, to be brothers than to be competitors—so perfectly obvious is all this that one sometimes feels like going out with Wisdom "into the top of the high places, beside the gates at the entry of the city, at the coming in of the doors," and crying with her: "O ye simple, understand prudence, and ye fools, be ye of understanding heart!"

I have no doubt that we need and must have some better organization of labor;

forms that give larger room for the free play of brotherhood than those which now prevail—forms which shall invoke it and incorporate it. But first of all we must get the idea. We are transformed, we and our institutions, by the renewing of our minds, by getting new ideas. According to our faith it will be unto us. Not until we believe in brotherhood as the foundation of the industrial order shall we be able to find the forms which will express it.

Pauperism and crime are problems that confront us. How shall we eliminate the pauper, exterminate the criminal? Are there laws that can contrive it, forces that can achieve it? Repression, regulation of all sorts, have been tried; the tale of severities has been exhausted. We have flung to the pauper the dole which signified our superiority and his dependence: that was the denial of brotherhood. We have made the prisoner an outcast, by our obdurate resentments disowning him. Under this treatment paupers and criminals are multiplying apace. Is there not some better way of dealing with them? Does the law of brotherhood reach down to this level? Verily, it seems so. There was Lazarus at the gate of Dives; there was the thief on the cross. "Blessed are ye poor," said Jesus; "yours is the kingdom of God." "It was I," he said, "that you found in prison; that low-browed, brutal creature, whom you took by the hand and lifted up —that was I. If you had anointed vision, you could see some lineaments of me in that repulsive face."

So the law of brotherhood pledges us to these. The Son of Man came to seek and to save that which was lost. He did save them; he can save them; and so can we, if his mind is in us. Our fault, our shame, has been that the truth of brotherhood has been disallowed, to the pauper in our pride, to the prisoner in our hardness. We have suffered the one to grovel at our feet; we have forced the other to skulk and hide from our faces. Neither is the brotherly thing to do,—how far from it! Can we learn to lift the one to his feet and to put a brotherly arm about the other? Love can save them both,—not always, indeed, without some wholesome severities of discipline; but the love that exalts character and believes in the divine possibilities of manhood can save them both. And what a task it is to reach and save these degraded and sinking millions, to lift them up into manhood—a task how appalling in its magnitude, but in its possibilities how alluring to heroic faith!

And democracy! There it looms right before us, writ large, in letters of flame, on the clouds that hang above our horizon— the one social question which includes, for us, every other. Shall democracy endure ? Shall government of the people, by the people, for the people, live and flourish, or shall it perish from the earth ? A question of some consequence, one would say, to this nation at least, perhaps to some others! Do you say there is no question? I answer that over considerable spaces of this continent, for considerable portions of time, government of the people has ceased to exist. Do you pretend to say that you, even now, are living under a government of the people ? How much had the people of this State to do with naming the men who are now, by a fine fiction, said to represent them in the Legislature ? or with authorizing or inspiring the measures of that body ? Is it the people's will that the Legislature of New York has actually sought to do? Is it the people who make nominations and influence appointments and dictate legislation hereabouts? You know better than I. If there is any truth in current reports, there is some question as to whether democracy, government by the people, is anything more than a name. What we have is really government of the people by bosses,—*for* whom the present deponent saith not, though he has his suspicions. Glimpses are seen through a screen, which is becoming more and more transparent, of the flitting forms of monopolist and pluto-

crat playing into the hands of the political
imperator.　Because he has the power they
are ready to pay him heavily for immunity
and privilege—the privilege of laying tribute
upon the people; because he gets their
money he can debauch voters, and control
nominations, and keep himself in power.

Is there a remedy for this ?　There is;
and, strange as it may sound to many, it is
nothing in the world but the simple recognition of Christ's law of brotherhood.　For
Christ's law of brotherhood is the corner-
stone of democratic government.　Mr.
Lloyd is speaking with scientific accuracy
when he says that '' the Constitution and
laws of the United States are, however imperfectly, the translation into the language
of politics of doing as you would be done
by.''　The foundation of republican government is not, ''Every man for himself:'' it
is, ''Each for all and all for each.''　On any
other foundation it is theoretically impossible.　What are the great words?　Liberty,
Equality, Fraternity,—and the greatest of

these is Fraternity. No; you cannot leave
that out; if you undertake to build your
State on individual interest, bidding each to
seek his own, unmindful of his brother's
good, you will have—just what you do
have in too many places—the form of liberty
without the power thereof.

All that there is need to do, therefore, is
simply to recognize the fundamental principles on which our government rests, and
make our practice conform to our theories.
We have only to do what every demagogue
promises to do when he asks the votes of
his fellow citizens. Does he not always
assure them that he will seek their welfare;
that he will make his own interests subordi-
nate to the service of the people? It is not
probable that they always believe him, but
he would not dare to say anything else.
He knows, and they know, we all know,
what the ideals of a democracy are. That
every man is a brother man; that there are
no privileged classes and no servile classes;
that the strong shall not aggrandize them-

selves by exploiting the weak; that all shall see that each has the opportunity of manhood,—this is democracy; the Christian doctrine of brotherhood lies at the base of it. We have only to clear our minds of cant and live up to our principles; that is all. We have got the idea; our creed is sound enough; the only trouble with us is that we so imperfectly realize it. Instead of using the power of all for the equal service of all, we have too often permitted the strong to monopolize power and to use it in the oppression of the weak; we have legalized and fostered gigantic egoisms whose purpose it is to lay tribute on the people. All this is in despite and defiance of the first principles of brotherhood. What we have to do is to repent and do the first works; to make our democracy mean, not monopoly nor autocracy, but government of the people, by the people, for the people.

" But have not the people all the rights that law can give them?" you may be asking. "Why do they not protect themselves ? And if they do not, who can save them ?"

Yes, I answer; they have all the rights that law can give them; and the issue shows us how weak the law is for the enfranchisement of humanity. Something more than legal privilege is needed: the wisdom and the will to use it rightly are needed also. If the ballot were a weapon of self-defense —which is about the highest idea of it that some people entertain—it would avail very little to millions of our voters, for they would not know how to use it for their own protection. Very dim, indeed, are the conceptions of its meaning entertained by great multitudes of those who are intrusted with it. I asked Mr. Reynolds, one day, how many of those swarming tribes and tongues on the East Side of New York had any idea of citizenship. "Well," he said, "most of them have found out that a vote is worth something—that they can get money for it." That, alas! is the first lesson in politics that a great many of them learn,—the only lesson, I fear, that multitudes of them ever have learned. And it is this that makes the problem of our democracy so serious. A democracy it is not when such elements largely enter into its constituencies. The men who can thus be manipulated by demagogues are not standing with us upon the level of brotherhood; they have sold their birthright, the badge of their political manhood; they have consented to become the underlings of bosses and the tools of the conspirators against liberty. If we have not the power to prevent this, we shall not wait long for the unrolling of the scroll of flame on which the words of doom are written. Listen to this solemn warning of the man who fell the other day fighting against the despotism of the boss:

" When there is general patriotism, virtue, and intelligence, the more democratic the government the better it will be; but when there is gross inequality in the distribution of wealth, the more democratic the government the worse it will be; for while rotten democracy may not in itself be worse than rotten autocracy, its effect upon national character will be worse. To give the suffrage to tramps, to paupers, to men to whom the chance to labor is a boon, to men who must beg or steal or starve, is to invite destruction. To put political power in the hands of men embittered and degraded by poverty is to tie firebrands to foxes and turn them loose amid the standing corn; it is to put out the eyes of a Samson and to twine his arms around the pillars of national life."

What shall be done about it? Shall we take this power from those who are not fit to use it? That is not an easy thing to do: there are barricades and dynamite along that road. The only way that I can see is to lift these multitudes up to the levels of citizenship; to deliver them from the thralldom into which, in their pitiful ignorance, they are selling themselves, into the manhood which is their heritage. Our brothers they are by right divine; we must redeem them, and make them worthy of the honors of brotherhood. There is no salvation for our democracy unless we can save them. It is a vast undertaking, no doubt; but how simple it would be if all who profess and call themselves Christians would but gird themselves for the work of realizing here on the earth the brotherhood which He came to found!

So it all comes back to this at last. Of all our social questions, this is the one: Do we believe in Christ's law of brotherhood ? Are we willing to recognize it as the fundamental law of all our social life, and to test all our methods, all our institutions, by it ? Of course there are millions of people in the world—Christians not a few, so called—who do not believe what Jesus told us about the Father, who flatly deny it all. When there was only one man in the world, they say, God was the Father of that one; but before there were two he had ceased to be the Father; the fall of man was a fall out of sonship into something else—strangerhood or alienship. Man may become a child of

God if he will repent and be converted;
until that change passes upon him, he must
not say "Our Father." And if we are not
the sons of God, then, of course, we are not
brothers. What are we? Competitors, I
suppose; there is no better word. It is on
this assumption that most of our theology
and our political economy has been built.
Here, just here, is the tap-root of most of
our social disturbances. The whole creation
groaneth and travaileth together, waiting
for the manifestation of the sons of God,—
waiting for the truth to shine out, as the
lightning shineth, from the one end of the
heaven to the other, that men are the
children of God, brothers by birthright,—
not foes, not strangers, but helpers one of
another.

Fellow men, we must believe it! What
is the good of disputing it and fighting
against it any longer? Has not the law of
strife wrought woe and desolation long
enough? Sometimes it seems to me that
the day of the great revelation cannot be

very far off. When we see selfishness in the industrial realm climbing into the colossal plutocracies that crush individual rights and lay their palsying hand on all our liberties; when we see selfishness in the State usurping all powers, and using the people as the tools of its vast malefactions, it seems to me that we are witnessing a demonstration of what selfishness, when it is finished, bringeth forth, which ought to convince the world that there must be some better rule of life. There is something so much better, so much nobler, waiting for us all, and not far away! How rich and strong and happy we might be, if we would only believe in it, and lay hold upon it with the faith that worketh by love! What possibilities are before us as soon as we learn that life means love!

"We are to become fathers, mothers," says Mr. Lloyd, "for the spirit of the father and mother is not in us while we can say of any child that it is not ours, and leave it in the grime. We are to become men, women, for to all about, reinforcing us, we shall insure full growth, and thus insure it to ourselves. We are to become gentlemen, ladies, for we will not accept from another any service we are not willing to return in kind. We are to become honest, giving where we get, and getting with the knowledge and consent of all. We are to become rich, for we shall share in the wealth now latent in idle men and idle land, and in the fertility of work done by those who have ceased to withstand but stand with each other. As we walk our parks we already see that by saying 'thine' to every neighbor we may say 'mine' of palaces, gardens, art, science, far beyond any possibility to selfishness, even the selfishness of kings. We shall become patriots, for the heart will know why it thrills to the flag. Those folds wave the salute of a greater love than that of the man who will lay down his life for his friend. There floats the banner of the love of millions, who, though they do not know you and have never seen you, will die for you and are living for you,—doing in a thousand little services unto you as you would be done by. And the little patriotism which is the love of the humanity fenced within our frontier will widen into the reciprocal service of all men. Generals were, merchants are, brothers will be, humanity's representative men.''

That is part of what it means—a little, a very little, of all that it means. And the world is waiting wearily to see it, to walk in the light and joy of it.

I think of that morning on the shore of Galilee, where, after his resurrection, our Lord appeared in the early dawn to the disciples who had toiled all night and taken nothing. '' Children,'' said the Master, '' have you aught to eat ? They answered him, No. And he said unto them, Cast the net on the right side of the boat, and ye shall find. They cast therefore, and now they were not able to draw it for the multitude of fishes.'' If through the long night of the centuries the toilers on the sea of life have taken less than they hoped for, may it not be because they have sought their gains on the wrong side of human nature— on the side of selfishness and strife ? And is it not his voice—the voice of the Son of Man—that now, in the dawning of a better day, we hear bidding us cast the net on the other side; to believe that love is wiser than craft, and that the hand that is open to give will forever hold more of the good of life than the hand that is clenched to keep ?

The Church of the Future.

WILLIAM J. TUCKER.

VI.

⯈be Cburcb of tbe ⯈uture.

By the Rev. WILLIAM J. TUCKER, LL.D.,[1]
President of Dartmouth College.

I ASSUME that you are quite as well aware
as I am that the subject which you have
assigned to me is full of temptation.
Happy is the man who can discuss the
Church, even the Church of the future,
without "falling into many foolish and
hurtful" disputations "which war against
the soul." I make no attempt to avoid the
difficulty, except it be to affirm, at the out-
set, our agreement with all believers in
Christ at the essential point.

---

[1] Plymouth Church, Brooklyn, Thursday evening,
November 11, 1897.

The Church of the future must be the Church. In this, I say, we are all as clearly agreed as are those who are known by distinction as " churchmen." The revolt against ecclesiasticism on our part has never led us to accept any weak and shifting substitutes for the Church of Christ. We have never abandoned our right in the common possession. The right to possess is the right to inhabit, the right to appropriate, the right which may deepen at any time into the obligation to reform. These are still our rights in the Church.

The significant fact to-day within the Church is the strength of the movement toward Christian unity among the more advanced types of Protestantism. It is futile for us to say that we, who are Protestants of Protestants, are happy in the mere fact of denominations and sects. If the sect is the price of freedom, we will pay it. If it is the permanent price, we will pay it to the end. But a sect, a denomination, a communion, whatever name you may use to declare or to disguise the fact of a part, and however that part may have been dowered with freedom, does not represent our full idea of what the Church ought to be, or our full faith in what the Church will be. It does not express our present feelings and desires. The hymns we sing are the hymns of the Church universal. We would not tolerate a sectarian hymn. The saints whom we appropriate are of all communions. The fact that some of them might have disowned us does not lessen our sense of ownership. We crave the largest possible fellowship among the living—possible within the limits of truth and honor. We are working the great federal idea as the best practical embodiment in our time of the unity of the Church. Nowhere, as I believe, is there a clearer conception of the fundamental idea of the Church, or a deeper sense of its meaning, than among those who are forced to stand for the dignity and rights of the churches. We accept to the full the distinction between a purely personal Christianity and the organic union of souls in Christ.

I pause to emphasize the distinction. I go back for a moment into the origins of Christianity. The first view we have of the Christian Church is that of the group around the table of Christ. John alone with Jesus would have represented discipleship, but not the Church. The Church is a society of which the original and simplest form is the group. So we have the outward growths of the Church—first the group gathered about the person of the human Christ, then the society organized in his name to commemorate his sacrifice and to bear witness to his resurrection, and then the community springing up on every hand permeated with his Spirit, and striving to exemplify his teachings. We are, of course, back of the great formalities of the Church. Nothing has as yet been conventionalized. The newness, the absolute strangeness of the life of the Church gave it its first unity. The unity of the early Church was built up on

the rare and seemingly impossible virtues,
like the forgiveness of enemies. A man
could not be a Christian in those days and
be like anybody else outside his own kind.
The Church was a succession or aggregation
of groups of like-minded and like-hearted
men and women, made one by the incom-
ing of that Life which has mastered all, and
which had changed them in measure to its
likeness: every one of whom could say,
" The life which I now live I live in the
faith of the Son of God who loved me and
gave himself for me."

One fact explains the origin of the Christian Church. The Spirit of Christ, spreading from life to life, made some form
necessary to express and develop the col-
lective life. How much of organization,
how much of ritual, how much of creed, was
the open and varying question. It is still.
It is one of the questions which confronts
Christianity as it enters each new age, and
each new race, and every new stage of
Christian civilization. And there seems to

be but one answer to the question from the spiritual side: no more organization or ritual or creed than the Spirit of Christ can inform and utilize; up to that limit, perfect liberty.

I assume that the celebration of the half-century of this church, so wonderful in its history, is a fit occasion for the reaffirmation of faith in the Church universal, the holy Catholic Church. The life of this particular church, which stands out with so much distinction, if you will with so much separateness, has no other source than that which feeds the whole body of Christ. And yet, because of its history, because of its distinctive qualities, because of the very contrast which it has to offer, it has the right to ask its own questions, to hold its own opinions, to cherish its own faith about the Church of the future. Especially it has the right to ask why so many and so great divergencies from the common type are necessary, why must there be so many separate communions and individual churches which bear so conspicuously the stamp of independence.

Or, to change the form of the question and extend it, why is the Church at large so far away from the realization of its own working unity, unable as yet to think or act or worship in any real spiritual unity, to say nothing of uniformity ?

I address myself, in what I may further say, to the answer to this question. The answer, to my mind, is twofold; a part of it is written in history, a part of it is being wrought out before our eyes.

First, the Church can never realize its own working unity—the Church of the future cannot be any other than the Church of to-day—until it makes a sufficient place in its life for freedom, particularly for intellectual freedom. The Church for a long time attempted to secure unity by ignoring and suppressing freedom. The result was Protestantism. The same result is sure to follow to-day, and always, even when the attempt is made in our Protestant communions. Protestantism is not a history. It is a principle. We make no progress by celebrating historic events. We make progress by applying principles. Now, the principle of Protestantism is one *essential* factor in the unity of the Church. The rights of conscience, of private judgment, of free investigation, have gained a standing which cannot be withdrawn. It is absurd to conceive of the Church of the future as existing without them. How long it will take to win for them complete recognition no one can tell. Sometimes we are amazed at the apparent backwardness of the Church. Examples come to our knowledge which we cannot ignore. But if you are recalling, as I speak, the various attempts which have been made during the past years to restrict the honest freedom of thought or inquiry, we must also remind ourselves of the uniform failure of these attempts.

Resistance to the principle of religious liberty is intrenched for the most part in scant minorities. All the more advanced

communions are agreed in theory and fact
—for nearly every one has now been put to
the test—that the Church must make room
for the largest and freest growth of the
individual. We accept no standards which
lower the stature of the Christian man.
Rather than allow this, even in the assured
interest of unity, we will wait, wait " until
we all come in the unity of the faith and of
the knowledge of the Son of God unto the
perfect man, unto the measure of the
stature of the fullness of Christ."

But this part of my answer need detain
us no longer. It has been written in history. The Church of the future must be
free. It has bought its freedom with a
great price. I have no doubt about the
coming freedom of the Church. My doubts
and fears all center around the second part
of my answer. I have reserved, therefore,
time for its larger presentation.

The Church can never realize its working
unity, it cannot realize itself, until it is willing, and until it knows how to lose itself in

the life of humanity. Do you say that this
answer is so broad that it is vague ? Then
let me bring you back to the law of Christ,
as true to the Church as to the individual,
"Whosoever will save his life shall lose it,
and whosoever will lose his life for my sake
shall save it." This was the law to which
Christ subjected himself, and of which he
reaped the benefit. And the marvel of his
life was not simply the willingness, it was
still more the ability, one may almost say
the skill, to lose himself in humanity.
Herein lay, of course, the mystery of the
Incarnation, but equally, also, the clear and
fine action of the whole after-life. With
what restraint he kept himself from all partial and false assumptions of authority,
ecclesiastical or political! How consistently
he refused to be drawn aside into secondary
and passing issues! With what tremendous
steadfastness he held to the one course which
would take him completely, absolutely, and
forever into the life of men! Call to mind
the glowing words of St. Paul as he tries to

tell the process and then to show the reward. ''Who, being in the form of God, thought it not a thing to be desired to retain his equality with God, but made himself of no reputation and took upon him the form of a servant, and, being found in fashion as a man, he humbled himself and became obedient unto death, even the death of the cross. Wherefore God hath highly exalted him and given him a name which is above every name, that at the name of Jesus every knee should bow, of things in heaven, and things in earth, and of things under the earth, and that every tongue should confess that he is Lord, to the glory of God the Father.''

There are limits to the imitation of Christ, but who will doubt that it is the supreme business of his Church to reproduce his spirit and his method and his purpose in the world? What is the Church put into the world for, except to lose itself in the life of the world, that it may thereby save its own life and that of the world?

This is not the loss of identity; it is the exact opposite of all compromise or concession; it is simply the complete and joyous surrender of itself to the one end and object of its existence. But the history of the Church shows a constant struggle between the two policies, the policy of saving and the policy of losing. Only in the great moods of the Church has it risen to the sublime conception or practice of Jesus, of losing its life in that of humanity. Such was the mood of the martyr period, when the Church poured out so fully its life-blood into the heart of the world. Such was the mood of the great reforming period, when the Church had found out that it could do better for the world than to suffer at its hands, and straightway undertook to give it liberty and law and righteousness. Such was the mood of the period which ushered in modern missions, expressed in the remarkable saying of young Mills to his comrades, "We ought to carry the Gospel to dark and heathen lands, and we can do it if we will.'' And such I believe to be the mood into which the Church is beginning to rise, in the person of its choicer souls, by which it is fulfilling the task of entering into the real life of the modern city, identifying itself with the humanity which has no voice but a cry, or a grievance, or a threat, and trying to interpret man to man.

But over against these greater and rare moods is the common and commonplace mood of the Church, which is always expressed in one way or another in the policy of saving its own life,—a policy of exclusion, of separation from the life of humanity, a policy of using the world for its own aggrandizement. I do not put in evidence the degenerate and worldly periods of the Church. I call your attention to the very theories and doctrines which the Church has tried to make itself believe, and trained its children to believe, based on the exclusiveness and separateness of its life from that of the common humanity; the appalling doctrine of the arbitrary election of the few against the many, or the weak and illogical theory of the hopelessness of the many, for want of a present and visible connection between a Universal Saviour and those for whom he died. I call your attention to the ease with which the Church in any community follows the lines of social classification and becomes identified with men in classes. I call your attention to its contentment with works of charity and rescue, which reach the few, instead of concern about changing the conditions which affect all. I call your attention to the want of a steadfast and united effort and struggle in regard to those interests which are wrapped up in the life of the city and the State. I make mention of these things, not in the way of an indictment against the Church, for that is far from our present business, but that we may not underestimate the problem before us. It is nothing less, as I have said, than to cause the Church to believe in and to carry out the policy of losing itself in the life of humanity. The

hopeful sign is that the idea is coming in
and beginning to shape itself into a faith.
This is the vision of the latter day, not of
a Church saved out of the world, but of a
world redeemed by the Church. In one of
his more daring utterances Dr. Dale once
spoke of the motive which impelled Christ
to come into the world. It must have
been, he said, that he somehow felt that his
fortune was bound up in the fortune of
humanity. Surely this is true of his
Church. It cannot be much better in the
end than it can succeed in making the
world. The great object for which it longs
and prays touching its own life will not
come about directly, but indirectly through
its service in the life around it. The
Church is intent upon unity. That will not
be brought about by any force working from
within, not by agreements or adjustments
or concessions or compromises. The unity
of the Church will come in only through the
brotherhood of man.

And now, do you ask me how this idea is

to be realized, how this policy is to be carried out by the Church of saving its life by losing it in the life of humanity? I can refer only to certain sure agencies. First, the wise and fearless use of truth. Emerson used to say, "He who helps one man helps one man; he who tells the truth helps mankind." The supreme power of the Church is the power to tell the truth. This is other than charity, except as the truth is told in love. But the truth to be told must be known, and to be known it must be sought out. Courage without knowledge is mere audacity. It may exhibit the man, it will not help the truth. I believe that the power of the Church of the future will rest more rather than less upon its pulpit. A truth-knowing, truth-loving, truth-telling pulpit will carry the truth into the deepest and most remote places. So this Church, through its pulpit, carried the truth of the rights of man down into the heart of the Nation, and out into its uttermost parts. No other agency could have wrought so

mightily against slavery and for freedom as
the plain, uncompromising, unceasing truth.
Truth which is timely will bear iteration.
Blow on blow will tell. Appeal after appeal
will be heard. The truth will prevail.
That is our hope in present moral issues as
in respect to the past, if only we can get a
like hold upon the truth, the whole truth,
and nothing but the truth.

And next to the persistent use of the
timely truth I put the training of the social
conscience. The modern Church has thus
far been brought up in individualism—a
strong and wholesome discipline, but not
sufficient for present conditions or for those
which are impending. It is our constant
complaint that corporate action is not as
responsible as individual action. We say
that the same man cannot be depended
upon to act with others as he will act when
alone. Perhaps we ought not to expect
that he will. Nevertheless, the fact remains
that corporate responsibility must bear some
proportion to the tremendous advance in

the absorption of individual activity into corporate activity. You have lost the individual; how are you going to follow him with individualism ? Individual responsibility is becoming capitalized; how are you going to get at the moral value of the new capital ?

Or, carry the thought over into our social and civic obligations. In the old days of Boston, in the time of its transition from a great village into a city, the citizens organized themselves into a Watch and Ward Society. They took turns in patrolling the streets. Of course this could not last. A city means delegated authority, the creation of departments to do certain things, and then usually the organization of societies to see that they do them. This is the process by which we divest ourselves of individual responsibility,—not by denying it in the first instance, but by putting the exercise of it at a further and further remove from us, till at last with this removal of responsibility there comes in the gradual loss of senti-

ment, of feeling, and even of shame. I
suppose that it would be as hard for the
average citizen of this city to repent of his
share of its sin as for a man trained in the
New England theology to repent of the sin
of Adam. He doesn't know how to do it.
His mind, as now trained, is not capable of
working that way.

What we want, in the Church at least, is
a habit of mind which will correspond to
present facts and conditions. It is useless
to confront new and obstinate conditions
with old habits of thinking, or with unused
sensibilities. Every great movement, from
the Reformation down, has demanded and
created for itself an appropriate habit of
mind and of conscience. No great headway
can be made until this demand has been
complied with. When once the present
demand has been met, and a habit of mind
has been created which will express itself
steadily and rightly through sensitiveness
to others, through responsibility for things
held in common, through what we must

call, in spite of its philosophical vagueness, "the social conscience," the Church will have made a sure advance in the art of losing itself in the life of humanity.

And, finally, I urge, as the great incentive to the realization of this end, the acceptance of the idea itself, the announcement of it, the assumption that it is here and at work in the life of the Church. We prepare ourselves for this conception of the Church by appropriating it and using it. When the Baptist came among men, he said, "Repent, repent! the kingdom of heaven is at hand." When Jesus came, he said, "The kingdom of heaven is at hand," it is here, "repent and believe the Gospel." Not preparation for something to come, but participation in something present! Let us recognize every effort on the part of the Church, however humble it may be, to lose itself in the life of humanity. Let us hold it up as the great conception. This is not an idea to be taken up for a mission, or a social settlement, or a crusade; it is some-

thing to be made the business of the great
Christian majority. The Church cannot go
on with its advanced work under present
contradictions, here and there a few souls
the world over losing themselves in the life
of others, and everywhere else the Church,
in one way or another, building itself up out
of the world. Why have we come to a halt
in foreign missions ? Chiefly, I believe,
because we are beginning to be ashamed,
through all our Christian nature, of our
unsanctified materialism. The nations have
found us out, and we know it. They have
explored Christendom, and what impresses
them most is the vast amount of unapplied
Christianity. Here, then, is the immediate
work of the Church. Here lies the ready
task of the new Christianity, to set Christendom in order—its cities, its industries, its
society, its literature, its law. In so doing,
we again make the Gospel the power of
God unto salvation to every one that be-
lieveth, to the Jew first, and also to the
Greek.

The Church of the future—it must be the Church. Upon that we are agreed. Whatever may be our interpretation of its authority, we maintain the fact without doubt or qualification.

The Church of the future will be free. That is a safe prophecy. There will be room in it not only for men themselves, but for all that they know and believe and hope for. Like the city seen in vision, it will stand open wider and wider, that men may bring their glory and honor in to it.

Will the Church learn to lose itself in the life of humanity? Will it at last catch the sublime secret of its Master and make that its own? Who will venture to affirm so much? Who dares to hope for less?

Retrospect and Outlook.

CHARLES A. BERRY.

VII.

Retrospect and Outlook.

By Rev. CHARLES A. BERRY, D.D.

DR. ABBOTT AND CHRISTIAN FRIENDS:
—I have so far thrown my life into the life
of this congregation as to know that it
would be foolish, not to say cruel, were I to
detain you at this time of night; I will content myself with one or two remarks suited,
I think, to a jubilee occasion.

The first is that the man or the institution
which has ceased to think of or care for
yesterday is "no good" for to-day or to-
morrow.

---

[1] After President Tucker's address, Dr. Berry was
asked to close the exercises with a few remarks,
which are here given as taken down by the stenog-
rapher.

The second is that the church which thinks too much about itself, about its history, about its principles, about its traditions and aptitudes, is going to waste its whole life in that kind of thinking, and will stop short of fruitful action.

And my third remark is that the church which honestly and sincerely finds fault with itself has infinite promise of usefulness and progress in the days to come.

These three remarks have germinated in my mind while listening to the address of President Tucker. I could have imagined I was at the Congregational Union of England and Wales, hearing such scriptural, constructive doctrine of the Christian church.

I have been at many meetings to-day, and at one of them two speakers, broad, catholic-minded, cultured men, announced themselves as "Churchmen." I could have understood that in England, where we have grown into a loose use of language; but in America, where you are always precise and accurate, where you do not talk "newspaperese,'' I was amazed to hear the term used, as they used it, to characterize a single denomination.

With some others, I have set myself in England to recover the term ''Churchman'' as the proper title of every man who has joined his individual Christian life with an organized Christian society. We are known by negative terms in England. You, I believe, have only one of those negative terms in America. We are known as Protestants, Nonconformists, and Dissenters. You, together with other great churches in this country, have only the first of those negative terms as descriptive of you.

I am not ashamed of being called Protestant: I glory in it; and I glory in it the more because there is a large school of thought growing up in a particular church in England which is trying to banish the word and to banish the thing. And I am proud as any man can be of a great heritage in the name of Nonconformist and the name of

Dissenter.   But while I use these terms for myself, and while I use them amongst my friends, I rise in indignant repudiation when either Catholic or Anglican flings those terms at me as descriptive of my position, and I claim to be as against them not only a Churchman, but a High Churchman.

The Protestant is a man who protests. What does he protest against?   He protests against the claim of a particular ecclesiastical dignitary to be the vicar of Christ on earth; that is what he protests against ultimately: and his protest is based upon this, that, when he has Christ himself, he stands in no need of a vicar of Christ. A vicar, as you know, is, etymologically and actually, one present who represents another who is absent.   Very well.   If a great church is content to say that the Master is absent and must have a vicar to represent him, that is its own lookout. But since we claim, and claim with good evidence of the truth, that we have a Master with us, then we protest against any man setting himself up to be Christ's vicar.

I have been at a good many jubilees lately; in fact, I feel quite at home at a jubilee. We have been having a Diamond Jubilee in England. You have not reached that yet: I hope you will, and I hope Dr. Abbott will be pastor. But at the real jubilee of Her Majesty's reign ten years ago, there was a great ceremony of thanksgiving at Westminster Abbey. I sat with others in the great west gallery and had full view of the whole scene. I noticed one thing very striking and very suggestive. You know, in England we do nothing without the presence of royalty; but, as the Queen cannot be everywhere, we have a pretty little device in the shape of what is called a mace, and this mace is representative of the official presence of the Sovereign. The House of Lords cannot sit in session unless the mace is set on the table, in suggestion of the fact that the Queen is representatively present. The House of Commons cannot

sit without its mace on the table. Nor
can the High Court of Justice. At this
jubilee service every one of these great
bodies brought into Westminster Abbey its
own mace, carried by its mace-bearer. But
when, from the magnificent composition on
the organ, specially written for that occasion, Dr. Bridge swiftly swept the chords
around, and struck the first notes of the
National Anthem, the crowd got up and
cried, "The Queen! The Queen!"—and
servitors hurried with cloths and covered
up these maces. The living Queen was
there; and the metal mace, which was but
symbolic, had become an offense and must
be covered up. So, when we have the living Christ with us, we cover up the mace-
vicariate, whether it be Romish, or Anglican, or Nonconformist. The living Christ
is what integrates our church life, and we
are happy when we have him.

Well, I might illustrate our English Non-
conformity and Dissent in similar terms, but
then I should be making a speech. Yet,

when all these little expositions of terms were over, I should come to this point, that these negative terms are but clearances to make a wide-open space, on which our positive, constructive church doctrine rears itself in architectural symmetry and beauty. We are Churchmen, and no negative term describes us; and I shall regret it with a deep, unspeakable regret if the churches outside two particular churches in this country ever consent to surrender that accurately descriptive term when speaking of their organized association in Christ and with each other.

Much has been said to-night about the Church of the Future. I was glad to hear it is going to be in a sense the Church of the Past and the Church of the Present improved. I cannot join in any wholesale criticism, still less denunciation, of earlier forms of church life, whether in England or America. It is true the work of the Church has been markedly individualistic, but then the whole life of the world during the last fifty years has been markedly individualistic, and the church has entered into the conditions of life around it, and at least has tried to make these individual men as good as they could be made. We have come to changed conditions to-day; and it is a right instinct that is aroused in the Church to make it alive to its social obligations and duties. But it seems to me that the difference between the work that lies behind us and the work that lies before us may be stated as the difference between *remedial* Christianity and *preventive* Christianity. That is to say, the social work of the Church in the past—for the Church has had its social work in the past, and has done it with more or less efficiency—has been to remedy the effects of evils which have been left to work themselves out and multiply themselves in fresh evil effects. To-day the Church has aroused itself to this: it is our business to strike deeper, to get at the roots of these evils and remove them,—and then we shall be under no necessity to remedy their effects.

For instance, take the various philanthropic agencies of the Church in the past. They have been the kindliest of human movements, and the total of their effects constitutes a story which should fill us with gratitude to God to-night—the philanthropies of healing, the philanthropies of emancipating, the philanthropies which have raised the whole tone of thought about women and children, about workers in our factories and toilers on the land and on the sea. But among all these philanthropies, the Church stopped short of striking down at that root of *selfishness*, which is the life-origin of all the mischiefs that are spread around us to-day. We have now opened our eyes to that fact; and under the guidance of great and consecrated thinkers it is becoming generally understood by our people that it is not sufficient to give a basin of soup and a blanket to some poor man, but the duty is to work for laws that shall prevent men from ever coming to such poverty.

Of course, among all this work we have
to remember—and at times I think some
of our social enthusiasts forget it or do not
sufficiently rate it at its significant value—
that much of the poverty, much of the sin,
much of the suffering in the world are due,
not to economic but to moral causes; and
the Church must never forget that, in striving to get at a new economy, she must,
alongside that effort, continue her old work
of trying to get at the lapsed and the fallen,
who, it may be, have lapsed and fallen
through evil conditions in the past, but who
are with us to-day and whose ills are turned
in sin and shame upon us. She must strive
at a gospel which aims at individual conver-
sion, and must do this as essential and
preparatory to that other and larger social
enterprise upon which we are graciously
entering to-day.

If I may be permitted to say so, without
even the distant suggestion of mere compliment, nothing in President Tucker's speech
struck so deep a chord in me as that in

which he reiterated his belief that the Church of Christ must lose itself in humanity. Yes, it must; but it must lose itself as a separate entity all the same. You plunge leaven into the meal; it is lost in the meal; it does its work in the meal: but it is able to do its leavening work because it is separate in nature from the meal which it is there to leaven.

And that is what we mean in England when we call ourselves "Separatists." It does not mean that we are gardens walled around. It does not mean that we are to live our own little life in our own little way, and get safely up to glory sooner or later. It means that we come away from the world in order to go into the world; we come away from the world to Christ in order that we may carry Christ back to the world. We build up our churches of men and women who have been alone with Christ; and then, when they have so separated themselves into communion with Christ, "Now," we say, "plunge right into the world and lose yourselves in the work of leavening the whole of humanity up to your own faith, your own love, your own joy and hope." Has it ever been your tragic lot to watch the rescue of a drowning man—how he tries to clasp his rescuer and so doom both to destruction? But the wise rescuer knows he must not let the poor, drowning creature touch him. He must get at him and grasp him, and not be grasped by him. It is so with the world and the Church. The Church must grasp the world, must grasp it by the firm grip of the strength it has discovered in Christ, must be separate from, in order that it may be one with, the world it means to save. Who would say that Christ, who identified himself with the race, had not to be separate from it? Separateness ran right through from the first day to the last of that unique life; but it was the separateness which I am trying, I fear vainly, to describe,—the separateness of one who finds the spring of his life elsewhere, and is consecrated to ideals far above the rush and movement of the life around him, but who out of that separateness gave himself to the race, and, as he was lost in it, lifted it to new vision and hope.

And so the Church of the Future, striking its roots deep into the past, above all striking its roots deep into the soil prepared by Him who promised to come and be in the midst of his people, must out of such rootage bear fruit more abundant, more beautiful, more fragrant, more satisfying than it has done in the past.

Dr. Abbott and Friends, it has been a sacrament to me to be at Plymouth at this jubilee. Two things have struck me. They are quite in the line of what I have been saying. The first is, that amid all the extraordinary services of this occasion you have steadily maintained your regular work,— not allowed it to flag. To me, one of the most beautiful things was that, though you were here for a special memorial service last Sunday morning, you admitted members to this church in the ordinary way at communion. It was typical of the whole attitude of this church to this jubilee: "We will rejoice, and we will sing special songs; but we will go on with our work." There seems to me great hope in that.

And a second point which has struck me is that, while you have been commemorating a great personality, a personality so contagious, so great, as to be felt beyond the sea not less than here, you have remembered your present duty and consecrated yourselves afresh to the work which lies before you. In that spirit, my dear friends, I pray you may continue. Continuing so, living the life of to-day, among the men of to-day, preaching the truth of to-day, there can but come upon you that blessing of God which maketh rich, that grace of Christ which, in proportion as it enables you to work for others, fills you with joy and satisfaction.

The Descent from the Mount.

LYMAN ABBOTT.

VIII.

The Descent from the Mount.[1]

By the Rev. LYMAN ABBOTT, D.D.

"And look that thou make them after their pattern, which was shewed thee in the mount."— *Exodus*, xxv. 40.

MOSES was accustomed from time to time to go away from Israel, into mountain solitudes, and there receive the inspiration which was to impel and the vision which was to instruct. Inspired and instructed, he came down from these mountain solitudes to tell the people how they were to live. Thus inspired and instructed, he laid the foundations of the Hebrew commonwealth;

---

[1] Plymouth Church, Brooklyn, New York, Sunday morning, November 14, 1897.

revealed to them the great political principles which have underlaid free governments ever since, the fundamental principles of social moral order, and the essential elements of vital spiritual experience. To-day it would be difficult to find a better and simpler statement of the fundamental principles of the social order than that afforded by the Ten Commandments. The Levitical code has long since passed away into oblivion, but the four elements of religious experience to which it gave expression still abide as the four fundamental elements of spiritual life—penitence, thanksgiving, consecration, and communion.

From time to time prophets and poets arise who bring to the world similar inspiration and similar vision: men with clear sight, who have perceived more clearly than most men what are the eternal verities; men of quickened hearts, who have more courage than most men to proclaim what they have seen; men of the larger hope, more audacious to believe that the ideals which they

have seen in the mountain-top can be realized in common life. Poets, we call these
men. The word poet means " maker."
The poet is the real maker of life, the real
creator, for he is the one who etches for us
what we are to make. Prophets, we call
them, because they speak for another, and
through them Another speaks forth the
truth—the truth of life coming from God.
These vision - experiences come to us in
our households, interpreted to us by the
prophets of our homes. Women, God makes
to be idealists. They see with clearer vision
than men, whose eyes are filled with dust,
and feel with more blessed assurances than
men, whose hearts are perturbed with the
perpetual conflicts of life. Blessed is the
man who can look back to the visions he
has received from his mother! Blessed the
man who walks with a guardian angel by
his side, who from time to time clears
away the dust that fills his eyes as well as
the perturbations that disturb his heart,
and helps him to see the true life and the

true God, through eyes he trusts in the woman he loves!

But not only through others — poets, prophets, wives, mothers — come these visions to us: they come to us directly and immediately. All healthful young men and young women have these vision-hours. They all love poetry; they all love novels, —not always the modern novel, which is very far from a portraiture of ideals, but novels and poetry which transcend all visible realities. All healthful young people love poetry and love good novels, because these appeal to their sense of vision. They see a better life than that by which they are surrounded; a better love than that which blooms by their side; a larger hope than that which animates the public men, the business men, the social life in which they walk. When the cynic tells them that they are young, and laughs at the hopes and visions of their youth, he is a liar: they are truth-seers. There is not a boy here to-day who does not sometimes see a vision of a

better life, nor a girl who does not sometimes feel herself drawn to something more
splendid than she has ever witnessed. These
are beckonings of God. This is the touch
of God upon the eyes that are blind, saying, Open your eyes and see, you that saw
not. Welcome these visions and truths.
In them God calls you unto the mountain-
top, that he may reveal to you the pattern
according to which life should be shaped.
And even in later life, from time to time,
we get these visions. Sometimes they
come through poet, through prophet,
through wife, through mother, through
memory of past experience; sometimes
they come we know not how. Tennyson
says—I quote his sentiment, not his words,
—"We walk in the valley, and the eternal
mountains are hid by the hills of time."
Sometimes we climb these hills of time and
see the eternal mountains,—and then, when
we come back again, are almost inclined to
discount our vision and put it from us as an
idle and fugacious thing. No, God has

called us to the mountain-top to show us a pattern.

Now there are two things that I want to say about these patterns, these visions. The first is, that we are not to stay in the mountain-top looking at them. We are not to think that because we have enjoyed a vision, we are religious. It is no more religious to enjoy a splendid vision of the truth than it is brave to enjoy reading Tennyson's "Charge of the Six Hundred." We can no more dwell in these than we can live in an architect's plans. When the plan is drawn, the house is to be built according to the plan. But the plan is not the house. When the inspiration of courage has been stirred in our heart by the charge of the Six Hundred, we are to do and dare and die, if need be; but the courage is in doing and daring and dying, not in reading the poem about doing and daring and dying. You cannot divide life into two sections, one secular and the other religious, and think you are religious because when the curtain

is raised and the drama is played before your
eyes you wipe the tears away from your
eyes under the pathos of it, or feel your
heart stirred with the splendid utterances of
the elocutionist. To be religious is to live
the drama of life, not to look at it; to act
the true life, not to hear it.

We are to build according to the pattern
in the mount; not merely stay and feast
our eyes upon it. Our noblest moments are
to be those that indicate to us what our life
should be. We are not to take counsel of
our more prosaic hours; we are not to be
guided by our more doubtful experiences;
we are not to sail by our guesses in the
hours when the fog environs; we are not to
walk by short-sighted expediencies in the
masmatic mists of the valley. Having
climbed the hills and seen the path, in that
very path which has been so witnessed to us
from the hilltop we are to walk. When
we have ascended our mount and the vision
has been given us and the pattern displayed,
we are to build according to that pattern,

and not according to some poorer and lower one.

Men say that these visions are impracticable. The only thing that is practicable is the highest. It is not true, "Whatever is, is right;" but it is true, "Whatever is right, can be." And it is for us, when we have gotten the vision of purity and truth and courage and righteousness, then to act it out in the real drama of our daily life. It is not the practical politician who can tell us what will make a prosperous nation: it is the poet. It is not the man who measures life by expediency who can tell us what will make prosperity either to the individual, the home, the nation, or the church: it is the prophet. It is not Aaron Burr: it is Charles Sumner. When we have been on the mountain-top, and have seen the vision, and our hearts have burned within us with a larger hope, and we have come down out of the mountain-top to engage in the ordinary vocations of our life, in the shop, the office, the home, we are to carry the memory of that vision with us and square our life to that. Never anything less. "Be ye perfect as your Father in heaven is perfect." We are not to say, "Ah, that is too much. I cannot be perfect." What if a mason should say, "You cannot have a perfectly perpendicular wall. I will let the house be crooked!" What if a plumber should say, "You cannot prevent a pipe from leaking, I will let the pipe leak!" That is not the kind of plumber or mason we want. We are to build to the plumb-line; and the ideal life is that by which we are always to test our conduct, measure our character, and guide and determine our living.

For the last week this church has been upon the mountain-top. I wonder how many have said to me, "What an uplifting time we have had!" My task this morning is no simple or easy one; it is so to bring you down from the mountain-top that your vision will do you good, not harm. If for this week you and I in our individual lives, and this church in its church-life, are to go on living the same life we lived before, with no deeper faith in God, no larger sympathy for our fellow men, no more vital spirit of self-sacrifice, no more living consciousness of a living Christ than we had before, it were far better for us if we had never gone up to the mountain-top.

It seems to me, as I look back upon these meetings, as though some divine mind had wrought on the mind of each speaker who has addressed us, and worked•them all to a common end and fashioned them all to a common message: Dr. Gordon declaring to us that there is but one Sovereignty in the world; Dr. Gladden telling us that we only conform to our Father which is in heaven when we are inspired by his love and count all men our brethren; Dr. Tucker saying to us that we cannot live this life of service and of love without sacrifice, and that we shall accomplish God's work in the world only as we lose our life that we may find life for others; and Dr. Berry encircling this

message by his addresses on Sunday morning and on Thursday evening, phrased in
the enunciation of the truth that the living
Christ in the heart of a living church is the
secret of its power—to know the living
God, to carry out the spirit of brotherhood,
to bear the cross.

This is the vision we have had. What
shall we do because of it ? How are we to
build our church-life and our individual
lives ?

There is but one Sovereignty in the world,
—Love. Not merely there is love in the
world; not merely there is sovereignty in
the world; but there is only one Sovereignty, and that Sovereignty is Love, only
one supreme Power, and that Power is
Love. How many men are there who
really think righteousness and purity and
truth are in the world conquering and to
conquer? But we shall have listened to the
services of the last week in vain if we do not
go back to take hold of life with a larger
hope, because of a profounder faith in love's

sovereignty. The iceberg breaks off from the glaciers in the North and floats downward to freeze the tropics. No flowers bloom upon it; no birds sing about it; no trees grow upon it; no life is nurtured on its bosom. But the great Gulf Stream embraces it, and little by little it dissolves, and takes on the heat of the stream, and is transformed into it and swept by it to Europe's shore, to baptize and to give it life. God is the Gulf Stream of history; and all coldness and selfishness, apostasy and falsehood and unrighteousness are yet to be dissolved in him. Iceberg after iceberg, ice-flow after ice-flow, floats down, but it floats on the bosom of God. God's breath is in the world, and it is a breath of spring. If when spring comes you find one corner of your garden still hard with frost, or still covered with snow, do you despair? You wait a little. Perhaps the time for planting has not yet come, nor of digging, but you know it will come, and you do not question that the breath of God is the breath of spring.

We shall have heard this message in vain if we do not take up our life with a larger hope.

And because God's heart is love and God's will is love, our work in it, God's work in the world, is a work of love. Last night if you had gone up Broadway at ten o'clock you would have seen a line of men at the corner of Tenth Street. You may see it any night. All night long that line is forming, men sitting on the curbstone, standing in procession, waiting until half-past four or five o'clock comes, that they may get a loaf of bread from the Vienna Bakery. So I am told, and I have seen the procession once. In the iron country of Pennsylvania are men — your brothers, my brothers—who have to work in the iron-mills twelve hours a day every day in the year. What time does that leave for home, for wife, for children, even for worship? In the city of New York and Brooklyn are women — your sisters, no stronger, no better able to bear the stress of life than your daughters and mine—who work in stores, the proprietors of which will not allow them to take a seat even when they are doing no work. In some of the States of this Union are children, six, seven, eight, nine years of age, dwarfing their minds and their bodies by toil and labor, when they should be at play or at school. These are some of the facts of our industrial life. They are not so bad as the facts of slavery. But they are not human brotherhood. It is not for this that Christ came into the world and lived and suffered and died. There is something more yet for us to do. Do you ask me how shall we correct these foul abuses? It is not mine to tell you how; not mine, at all events, to-day; enough for me to say this: There is a vision of human brotherhood that is far above this; a vision of human brotherhood which will give to all men enough; which will give to every man opportunity for self-development and self-culture; which will give to every husband time for his wife, and to every father time for his children, and to every man time for himself and for his God. That is the vision; and you and I are not to be content until that vision is realized. If we heard Dr. Washington Gladden's address here last Thursday night, in which, wisely refusing to discuss methods and plans, he simply held up the ideal of human brotherhood before us,—if we heard that, and then do not do something this very week to realize it, we had better not have heard. It is my duty to make human brotherhood a little more real in the *Outlook* office, and yours to make it a little more real in the relations with your domestic servants, and in your office and shop and store and factory, or your vision of human brotherhood has been worse than in vain. You are to come down from the mountain-top and build according to the pattern. Will you ?

We cannot do this without sacrifice. It costs something. It may cost a great deal. To some men, much; to some men, little.

But, at all events, if the law of human society is brotherhood, the law of church is more than brotherhood; it is this: "As I have loved you, that ye also love one another." It is service carried on to self-sacrifice.

What is a church of God ? It is not a body of men who come together for esthetic enjoyment, to listen to fine music and rejoice in a beautiful house, or to be pleased by oratorical display and splendid eloquence, or to be instructed and uplifted through the intellect and by discussion. It is not a body of men and women who come together, as on a mountain-top, to see divine and spiritual visions, and feel their hearts played upon as by the very fingers of God himself, and listen to the very music of the Celestial City. None of these things. Do you remember how John the Baptist sent to Jesus, and said, "Art thou the Messiah, or shall we look for another ?" and do you remember what he answered to the delegation? "Wait." And then he went on with his work. And the blind came to him, and he touched their eyes, and they went away to see; the lame came, and they threw away their crutches; the lepers came, and he put his hand upon their brow, and the scales fell off from their skin, and the fresh blood began to pulsate again in their veins. And then, when the work of healing was over, the people sat upon the ground, and he, standing on a little eminence, preached to them. And as he preached women wiped away the tears from their eyes; and men, despairing, looking upon the ground, lifted up their eyes and took the sunshine from Christ s face; and men and women who had sinned away their lives, and lost it all, took back new life from him and went forth with joy and hope in their faces. Then, when the sermon was over, he said to John's delegation, "Go, and show John again what things ye do see and hear; the blind receive their sight, and the lame walk, the lepers are cleansed, and the deaf hear, the dead are raised, and the poor have the glad tidings preached to them."

What is a church of Christ ? Do you want to know ? Do not go back to past history to find out what apostolic successions have come down through the centuries. Do not go to the record to find out what creed is written in the church-book. Do not go to the baptismal font to see, as Professor Swing has said, "whether water is applied to the candidate or the candidate is applied to the water." These are not the questions that determine what is a church of Christ. Go into the homes and lives of the church-members, into the mission work of the church, into the heart of the men of the church, into the congregations of that church, and see whether those that have been lame and footsore and weary are beginning to throw away their crutches and march toward the kingdom of God; whether those who have walked as they that are blind, or as seeing men as trees walking, are beginning to get their eyes open and to see the truth of God with celestial clearness;

whether those who have never heard anything but the beat of the hammer on the
anvil are beginning to hear the celestial
choirs; whether those who were sick and
struck through with leprosy are beginning
to be cleansed; whether those that were in
despair because of their sins are beginning
to look up and say, There is hope for me
within the kingdom. If so, that is a church
of Christ, whether it is Quaker or Catholic,
whether Episcopal or Presbyterian. What
is the church of Christ? The church that is
giving its service to men in the highest of
their being. Are you going to give yourself more to that service? Is your life going
to be a higher life ? Will our mission
chapels do better service ? Will our Sunday-
school be richer in its equipment ? Will
our individual lives be nobler ? Can you
throw away one crutch and walk with a
crutch and a cane ? This is the question.

You heard, and you applauded with a
silent appreciation, which is better than
hand-clapping, Dr. Berry's declaration that

the faith of this church is faith in a living
Christ. I was very glad—and I think I
speak for you as well—we were very glad
he did not come here to give us a message
about Mr. Beecher, but to interpret the message that he and we had received in past
times from Mr. Beecher. The living Christ
is the secret of the power of the church.
Moses came down from Mount Sinai, and
left the vision of Jehovah there, and coming down wore a veil upon his face, as Paul
tells us, that the people might not see the
reflected glory fade away. The centuries
passed by, and Jehovah came again, to live
in visible form, to walk a man among men;
and he took the disciples up with him into
the Mount of Transfiguration, and they
beheld him there in glory, as Moses had
beheld him in glory in Mount Sinai; but
when the cloud received those that talked
with Jesus, the revelation of Jehovah was
left, and the visible God descended out of
the mountain-top with the disciples. That
is the difference between Judaism and

Christianity. One is a memory; the other is a living experience.

We have been on the mountain-top; memories have been about us; we have seen, as it were, our own sainted dead; they have been with Christ and we with Christ, together. And now the cloud has received the sainted dead out of our sight, and we are coming down the hill into the valley where need and poverty and suffering and sin all are. Let us bring the living Christ with us, to inspire us, to bear the cross of Christ, not in gold upon our bosoms, nor in steeple on our church, but in our hearts and in our lives, that by our service we may gather all men to ourselves as brothers and to God as the All-Father through Jesus Christ his Son, never failing in our hope of the final result, because we believe that Love is the only Sovereignty.